On the Presidency

On Politics

L. Sandy Maisel, Series Editor

On Politics is a new series of short reflections by major scholars on key subfields within political science. Books in the series are personal and practical as well as informed by years of scholarship and deliberation. General readers who want a considered overview of a field as well as students who need a launching platform for new research will find these books a good place to start. Designed for personal libraries as well as student backpacks, these smart books are small format, easy reading, aesthetically pleasing, and affordable.

Books in the Series

On the Presidency, Thomas E. Cronin
On Foreign Policy, Alexander L. George
On Media and Making Sense of Politics, Doris A. Graber
On Thinking Institutionally, Hugh Heclo
On Ordinary Heroes and American Democracy, Gerald M. Pomper

THOMAS E. CRONIN

ON THE PRESIDENCY

Teacher, Soldier, Shaman, Pol

Paradigm Publishers
Boulder • London

Paradigm Publishers is committed to preserving ancient forests and natural resources. We elected to print this title on 30% post consumer recycled paper, processed chlorine free. As a result, for this printing, we have saved:

9 Trees (40' tall and 6-8" diameter)
3,217 Gallons of Wastewater
6 million BTU's of Total Energy
413 Pounds of Solid Waste
775 Pounds of Greenhouse Gases

Paradigm Publishers made this paper choice because our printer, Thomson-Shore, Inc., is a member of Green Press Initiative, a nonprofit program dedicated to supporting authors, publishers, and suppliers in their efforts to reduce their use of fiber obtained from endangered forests.

For more information, visit www.greenpressinitiative.org

Environmental impact estimates were made using the Environmental Defense Paper Calculator. For more information visit: www.papercalculator.org.

Published in the United States by Paradigm Publishers, 3360 Mitchell Lane Suite E, Boulder, CO 80305 USA.

Paradigm Publishers is the trade name of Birkenkamp & Company, LLC, Dean Birkenkamp, President and Publisher.

Library of Congress Cataloging-in-Publication Data

Cronin, Thomas E.
On the presidency : teacher, soldier, shaman, pol / Thomas E. Cronin.
p. cm. — (On politics)
Includes bibliographical references and index.
ISBN 978-1-59451-490-6 (hardcover : alk. paper)
ISBN 978-1-59451-491-3 (pbk)
1. Presidential candidates—United States—History. 2. Presidents—United States—Election—History. 3. Presidents—United States—Public opinion. 4. Political leadership—United States—History. 5. Public opinion—United States. I. Title.
JK528.C77 2008
352.230973—dc22

2008024747

Printed and bound in the United States of America on acid free paper that meets the standards of the American National Standard for Permanence of Paper for Printed Library Materials.

Designed and Typeset by Cheryl Hoffman

12 11 10 09 08 1 2 3 4 5

Contents

PREFACE

This book is for readers who are searching for a richer, more nuanced understanding of the modern American presidency.

As Americans and optimists, we yearn for heroic, patriotic, wise, and constitutional presidential leadership. Yet we also instinctively fear the abuse of power, frequently split our ballots, and regularly turn to the party out of power for change and hope.

We make it hard, if not impossible, for presidents to live up to our expectations, yet we are unforgiving critics when presidents disappoint us.

Do we expect too much? Yes, and we will continue to do so. Presidents have, on occasion, been tremendously consequential for this nation, yet we generally exaggerate the capacity of presidents to shape their times (see chapter 4). Some presidents overreach and resort to unacceptable manipulation as they try to live up to our lofty expectations (see chapter 5).

These chapters treat many of my favorite research and lecture topics. The presidency may be more than 220 years old, yet it is a constantly puzzling and changing institution. Those of us who teach and write on the presidency are challenged by its paradoxes and by how both the times and the individuals shape the office.

Political scientist Sandy Maisel and Paradigm vice president Jennifer Knerr invited me to join their inventive "On Politics" series, which specifically encourages writers to share personal and reflective essays. I am pleased and honored to do so. These chapters are that—personal reflections from a longtime presidency watcher.

I am indebted to scores of political scientists and historians who have in recent years developed a more extensive and rigorous scholarship on the presidency. I especially thank valued mentors and colleagues James MacGregor Burns, John W. Gardner, Michael A. Genovese, and Arthur M. Schlesinger Jr.

Special thanks to Lauren Arnest and Morgan Stempf for helpful editorial suggestions, to Kim-Marie Coon for skillful manuscript preparation, and to Jennifer Knerr and Melanie Stafford for their invaluable production guidance.

Finally, to Tania Cronin, thank you for your unfailing encouragement and for the art and music.

Tom Cronin
Colorado Springs
July 2008

Chapter One
Searching for the Perfect President

All presidents are blind dates.

—Jonathan Alter[1]

If God had wanted us to vote," reads an old bumper sticker, "he would have given us candidates." America has never had perfect candidates or presidents, nor is this likely. We yearn for qualities of judgment, character, experience, strength, agility, warmth, decisiveness, civic virtue, patriotism, and passion rarely found in any one person.

"[T]he office of president will seldom fall to the lot of any man who is not in an eminent degree endowed with the requisite qualifications," argued an optimistic Alexander Hamilton in 1788 as he urged ratification of the U.S. Constitution. "Indeed," Hamilton added, "there will be a constant probability of seeing the [presidency] filled by characters preeminent for ability and virtue."[2] However, a more realistic James Madison warned that "[e]nlightened statesmen will not always be at the helm."[3]

Presidential candidates always have the flaws associated with being human and politically ambitious. History suggests, too, that predicting who will become a great president is usually impossible, but this rarely inhibits our quadrennial searches for a new hero.

We should ask a lot of our presidential candidates. But most of us yearn for so many talents and qualities that it comes close to wanting "God—on a good day"—or at least a pleasant amalgam of Lincoln, the Roosevelts, Churchill, Mandela, Mother Teresa, and the Terminator.

When looking for a new president, we search for a leader who can bring us together and bring out the best in us. This is an especially tough assignment in a nation shaped by stalwart individualism and an abiding irreverence for politics and centralized government institutions.

Those we remember as "great presidents" are remembered primarily for their military victories and humanitarian vision, though—looking through our rose-tinted retrospective glasses—we remember even these presidents on their best days.

Consider these realities. We've had 14 presidents between 1920 and 2009. Maybe about three were successful. At least half a dozen failed in one way or another. Nixon was ingloriously forced from the office. Bill Clinton was impeached. The American voters vetoed four others when they sought reelection (Hoover, Ford, Carter, and Bush I). Two others (Truman and LBJ) wisely stepped aside rather than almost surely face voter rebuke in 1952 and in 1968.

The job of the American president is one of the toughest jobs imaginable. We doubtless expect too much of presidents, yet we are highly unlikely to ease up on them.

Presidential experts agree it's hard to tell in advance whether or not a presidential candidate will be an effective president. We are often told we need presidents with considerable experience. Yet three of our presidents who had the best prepresidency experience résumé were James Buchanan, Richard Nixon, and George H. W. Bush. James Buchanan, for example, served as state legislator, diplomat, secretary of state, and lengthy terms in both the U.S. House of Representatives and the U.S. Senate. Yet his impressive experience couldn't save him from becoming one of our worst presidents. Nixon and Bush I were better, yet had problematic presidencies. Harding and Hoover looked like presidents but failed miserably. Franklin Delano Roosevelt and Ronald Reagan were initially considered lightweights, yet they surprised most people. And three of our great wartime presidents had little or no military experience—Lincoln, Wilson, and FDR.

We would probably today rule out several of those who were successful. Take Lincoln, for example. He was decidedly unprepared to be president—so much so that even he wrote that he didn't think himself "fit for the presidency." Moreover he was homely and given to depression or at least prolonged bouts of melancholy. He had zero administrative experience and no foreign policy expertise. Yet not only did he rise to the challenges of his time, he is now widely considered the best president we ever had.

FDR's health and personal relationships would doubtless handicap him today if we knew in 1932 what we know now about him. This might also be true of John F. Kennedy and Bill Clinton.

Thomas Jefferson, the patron saint for the Democratic Party, is yet another president who might not make it to the White House if we knew then what we know now. Jefferson, it turns out, believed in black inferiority and opposed racial integration, yet fathered at least a few children with an attractive African American slave in his household.[4]

We are regularly disappointed in those who campaign for president in part because we so often measure them against an idealized composite of what our greatest presidents, and great world leaders, have done. We seldom compare current candidates with what past presidents looked like prior to becoming presidents.

It is part nostalgia, part oversimplification, and part dreaming. Former U.S. senator and past presidential candidate Bill Bradley faults his Democratic Party friends for constantly awaiting rescue by a "fairy-tale prince," a charismatic candidate who, he says, "is really a search for how you felt during JFK's time and after [his] assassination."[5]

"Every great president has been a captivating teacher," writes *Newsweek*'s Jonathan Alter. "They think big, instruct and illuminate us and elevate the public debate. Barack Obama in 2008 showed signs he could project his teaching voice in the theater of American politics, and yet we can never assume what will happen." Thus, even as he celebrated the Obama candidacy, Alter rightly cautions: "All presidents are blind dates."[6]

The U.S. Constitution requires only that a president be 35 years old, have lived in the United States for 14 years, and be a natural-born citizen.

The preamble to the Constitution says this new constitutional enterprise was established to form a more perfect union, establish justice, insure domestic tranquility, provide for the common defense, promote the general welfare, and, finally, secure the blessings of liberty.

Presidents are judged, and rightly so, on each of these public policy goals. It is exceedingly hard, however, to predict in advance how presidential candidates will do in each of these policy spheres.

American voters, understandably enough, have a tough and wide-ranging unwritten set of job specifications for those who are driven and presumptuous enough to run for the White House. At least two-thirds of probable voters in the United States have strong, or at least fairly strong, allegiance to one of America's two major parties. Most of these people prefer, other things being equal, that the next president be from their party. Partisanship is a powerful filter influencing how we assess those running for the office. Americans will discount a few personal attributes or political skills, even important ones such as character or executive competence, if a candidate in their political party is less endowed in this regard than those running in the other party or parties. Partisanship plays as great a role in judging who should be president as it does in the way we judge incumbents—and it has played an increasingly important role in how we have approved or disapproved recent presidents.[7]

Four realities should be understood before I elaborate on the list of qualities and skills I want in a top presidential candidate. First, it is almost impossible to know in advance what kind of a match a leader will be with his or her times. Presidents are very much the product of their times, shaped more than shapers. And we can never be sure that losing candidates might not have been even more successful than those who won. Thus, might Nixon, if he had won in 1960, have helped prevent our Vietnam disaster? Would Al Gore, if he had won the Electoral College vote in 2000, have been more adept than George W. Bush in waging our antiterrorist efforts? These are hard "what if" questions to answer, even as they are definitely worth raising. Most of us can agree, however, that at a bare minimum we want someone with character, judgment, political savvy, executive abilities, and a strategic sense for policy innovations.

Second, and something we often underestimate, is whether or not the person is electable. Electability is crucial. The person who wants to be president has to have a passion for the job, a passion for politics, and above all a magical ability to attract passionate followers. Without those a would-be president will not only fail to lead but fail to win election in the first place. That eliminates most people—including most people in public life.

Every four years we wonder if there isn't some way we could lure talented people from outside of politics to run for the White House. Dwight Eisenhower is illustrative, although he was a career public servant. More recently Ross Perot, Ralph Nader, General Wesley Clark, and New York City mayor Michael Bloomberg are examples. And what about Oprah Winfrey, Stephen Colbert, Lou Dobbs, Steve Jobs, or Tom Brokaw? Most of the time these hypothetical or failed candidates remind us that experienced politicians are not so inadequate after all, and that the presidency ought not to be an on-the-job training place for untested celebrities or mavericks.

We justifiably look at candidates with an unforgiving eye, but perhaps we are unfair with pop quizzes, trick questions, secretive stalking stakeouts, and denunciation of candidates for committing sins many of us are guilty of. We have, many analysts conclude, come close to having turned our presidential campaigns into freak shows.[8] The invidious mudslinging, innuendo attack ads, and blogosphere antics make it less and less attractive for anyone to run.

My third cautionary note is that what Americans look for in their next president is often shaped by what they haven't liked in the current or past few presidents. In a way, we often devise in retrospect a list of qualities we are not looking for in our next president. Thus after Herbert Hoover, Americans were doubtless looking for hope, not dour aloofness, and new economic initiatives, not the continuation of laissez-faire ruin. After Harry Truman's major problems with trying to conclude the Korean War, some of General Eisenhower's qualities looked attractive indeed. After the imperial presidency tendencies of the LBJ and Nixon period, Jimmy Carter's perceived sincerity, humility, and pledges about honesty were welcome. Yet after Carter's ineffectiveness on a number of fronts, a majority of Americans were ready for a change in both policies and leadership style. Hoover, Coolidge, Carter, and George W. Bush all championed their administrative talents, yet none proved to be great presidents. The lesson here is that our attitudes about what we want or what we determine to be "the right stuff" needed to be president vary, sometimes considerably, depending on the success and especially the deficiencies of those who have recently been in the White House and the pressing challenges of the day.

Fourth, incumbency generally, though not always, benefits a president standing for a second term. Sometimes, indeed, it has helped win a landslide victory as it did in 1936, 1956, 1964, 1972, and 1984. Sometimes it may merely account for a reelection win (as in 1996 and 2004). But incumbents Hoover, Ford, Carter, and Bush I lost despite incumbency. And Harry Truman and LBJ, both of whom initially wanted to run one more time, were prohibited from doing so by their failed incumbencies. On balance, presidential incumbency, although often an asset, is less of an asset than it is for members of Congress and state governors.

My list of what we should be looking for in candidates is divided into personal attributes and political skills. Inevitably there is overlap. I encourage everyone, scholars and citizens alike, to formulate their own criteria. It's an instructive and frustrating exercise, for we plainly want a lot, and we catch ourselves listing contradictory aspirations: principled moral leadership and hardheaded realism; supremely self-confident yet humble, empathetic listeners; statesmanship and political cunning. In fact, we want our presidents to be magicians and jugglers who can change and adapt to the constantly new and often unexpected circumstances (like 9/11) that they must confront.[9]

Here is an additional challenge for list-makers. Most of the qualities or skills we want are desirable only up to a certain extent. Thus, for example, we want drive and ambition—but not someone who is compulsively or recklessly driven. We want empathy and humility, yet this too can be overdone. A president, I will argue, occasionally needs to be cunning—yet too much of that can be fatal. All of us want a good listener, yet one who dithers overly long threatens to become a Hamlet. Presidents have to act, and they almost always must do so with incomplete information.

Personal Attributes

- Character/Honesty/Authenticity
- Courage
- Ambition and Drive
- Optimism
- Strength and Toughness
- Learner/Listener
- Self-Confidence
- Understanding (and Liking) People

Political Skills

- Political Savvy
- Strategic Thinker
- Coalition Builder
- Morale Builder/Capacity to Inspire
- Persuasive Communicator
- Stagecraft Performance Skills
- Executive Competence

Character and Honesty/Authenticity

Honesty usually tops the charts when Americans are asked what they want in a president. And this is especially the case after four decades of notable presidential deceptions, from the Gulf of Tonkin episode through Watergate, Iran-Contra, the Lewinski affair, and justifications for starting the Iraq War, to name just a few.

We want presidents to be ethical individuals whom we can proudly hold up as role models for our children and grandchildren. A dispiriting number of Americans today readily believe the maxim that "all politicians are liars."

But the honesty, or character, factor is complicated. Presidents are just as human as the rest of us. Revelations both during and after presidents have been in office about adultery, bigotry, and duplicity justifiably kindle concerns and discontent. Someone once said that leaders and heroes shouldn't be looked at up close—and there is some truth to this, as to the old adage that "nobody is a hero to his valet."

Should presidents be moral leaders? Does a moral personal life imply that their leadership will in turn be moral in its conduct? And if so, what constitutes moral and ethical leadership?[10] "In the ideal world, every president would be the paragon of virtue," said former New York governor Mario Cuomo. "The reality is that no human has been able to reach the ideal of leadership in which they reflect the best of virtue all of the time. We don't trust politicians to be our moral arbiter. We'd like them to be. But we don't expect it."[11]

Many Europeans look to their leaders to perform as political leaders, not as role models. They say, in effect, that the sexual morals of leaders are their own business. The private lives of politicians, they say, should be off-limits to scrutiny—unless there is a clear connection with their public life and public work. One problem we have today, however, is that we don't permit presidents much of a private life. "I may be President of the United States," President Chester Arthur once complained, "but my private life is nobody's damned business." That's wishful thinking in our day.

Another European saying has political leaders quipping snarkily that if the people want a sense of moral direction they should turn instead toward their bishops. Yet, as Americans have learned, the flaws and hypocrisy of charismatic preachers (such as Jimmy Swaggart and Ted Haggard) can be every bit as dubious as some of JFK's and Bill Clinton's personal escapades.

JFK aide Ted Sorensen writes of his sometimes philandering White House boss that the qualities of an ideal husband and an ideal president are not the same, explaining:

> Was JFK a moral leader? An American president, commander in chief of the world's greatest military power, who during his presidency *did not* send one combat troop division abroad or drop one bomb, who used his presidency to break down the barriers to religious and racial equality and harmony in this

> country and to reach out to the victims of poverty and repression, who encouraged Americans to serve their communities and to love their neighbors regardless of the color of their skin, who waged war not on smaller nations but on poverty and illiteracy and mental illness in his own country, and who restored the appeal of politics in the young and sent Peace Corps volunteers overseas to work with the poor and untrained in other countries—was in my book a moral president, regardless of his private misconduct. Public officials should be judged primarily not by their puritanism in private, but by their public deeds and public service, by their principles and policies.[12]

Sorensen makes a decent case even if he, as the debater he once was, wants us to overlook the Bay of Pigs invasion and the several thousands of military "advisers" sent to Vietnam on Kennedy's watch.

Machiavelli famously wrote that leaders may on occasion need to do harm in the larger cause of national security. And this whole issue gets additionally complicated by asking whether we want to be led by someone who is morally pure yet politically ineffective or by someone who may be personally flawed yet brilliantly able to provide for the nation's security and provide social justice and economic prosperity. Take FDR as an example—he was also an imperfect husband and someone who in addition plainly said he would deceive and tell lies if this would help win the war.

An additional important matter is understanding the moral responsibility of presidents and other top officials in extreme situations. Was it moral to firebomb Tokyo in World War II, or drop atomic weapons on Japanese cities? What of the case of the "ticking time bomb" when a captured terrorist knows its location but might need to be tortured before yielding information that might save a city? Part of the challenge for presidents and similar top government officials is making the tough and often impossible choices no ordinary person would want to make. Political theorist Michael Walzer talks about these as "moral paradoxes" where sometimes the right thing to do may be morally or ethically wrong. As Walzer suggests, we want our leaders to know the rules, understand the rules, yet also "be smart enough to know when to break" the rules, yet to "feel guilty" when they do engage in rule breaking, which he adds, "is the only guarantee they can offer us that they won't break it too often."[13] So it is that presidents may on rare occasions break certain rules that apply to the rest of us, yet when they do so they must not just feel guilty, they must also fully justify their actions.

Americans understandably want presidents they can trust, who have a profound respect for others, for constitutional and ethical rules, and a compelling commitment to serve the public interest. We want and should insist on fair play, integrity, and not just a sense of decency—but a proven track record of treating all people respectfully.

We do so because honest, ethical leaders inspire all of us to higher levels of compassion, service, and justice.

Did the president, as Lincoln once suggested, "appeal to the better angels within us?" Did he or she embody the best in us as a nation and thus inspire us to live closer to our ideals?

Franklin Roosevelt famously described the presidency as "preeminently a place of moral leadership." Roosevelt was talking about the capacity to do good, the capacity of the president to be a liberating and freeing force for good in the country.

In the end, we judge presidents more by what they do than on who they are. Both are important, yet as noted above, we elect them to govern and not to preach on individual morality.

There are two important points we "know" about the relationship between character and leadership. First, private character is not always the best guide or predictor of public character and leadership effectiveness. And second, our preoccupation with scandals and human imperfections scares away some splendid candidates who understandably refuse to put themselves and their families through the ugliness of public witch-hunts and smear campaigns. Saintly presidents there never have been and never will be. Those with the drive, energy, and ambition to run for the presidency are doubtless in some ways even more human than most of the rest of us. Remember, too, the Zen adage: "Water that is too pure has no fish."[14]

Courage

Dictionaries define courage as a state or quality of mind, or spirit, that enables a person to face danger with confidence, resolution, and bravery; in effect, a capacity for rising to a challenge. Note, too, these dictionary synonyms: mettle, fortitude, resolution, tenacity, backbone, and guts. They all imply physical and moral stamina in the face of hardship or unfavorable odds.[15]

John F. Kennedy, when he was a U.S. senator, wrote a useful book profiling U.S. senators who defied partisan pressures and voted their consciences. Kennedy celebrated them as having the guts to become mavericks or independents even when the intense pressure of their parties or public opinion would have had them vote otherwise.

Biographer Jonathan Alter writes about FDR's bravery during one of America's darkest hours. Noting that FDR was certainly not a genius, Alter adds that there was no single quality shaping FDR in his celebrated hundred days that was exceptional. Yet FDR projected a fearlessness and a courage that lifted the spirits of the nation. "It was a magical alloy of attributes," writes Alter, "his ebullience after the dour Hoover, his theatricality upon entering the big stage, and his pragmatism in the time of destructive dogma."[16]

Historian Michael Beschloss celebrates courage in his book *Presidential Courage: Brave Leaders and How they Changed America, 1789–1989* (2007). Beschloss notes that the ancient Romans surrounded their young leaders with paintings and sculpture that celebrated civic duty and qualities of greatness. Beschloss's case studies of Washington, Lincoln, FDR, Reagan, Truman, and others are written to remind Americans, and future presidents, that we have had at least a few presidents who on occasion risked their popularity, even their lives, for vital, larger causes.

British Prime Minister Gordon Brown pays tribute to eight courageous individuals who, through their commitment and social conscience, advanced the great causes of their day. He celebrates Mandela, Martin Luther King Jr., Robert Kennedy, Dietrich Bonhoeffer (a German resister of Nazism), and Cicely Saunders, one of the founders of the Hospice movement.[17] Brown cautions that acts of courage have to be continually distinguished from acts of fanaticism. And this leads to questions such as: Was abolitionist John Brown at Harper's Ferry courageous or a fury-driven fanatic? Was George W. Bush's antiterrorist decision to invade Iraq a rash, reckless act of overreaction, or a noble and decisive act of courage? The haunting documentary *The Fog of War* (2003), which interviews former secretary of defense Robert S. McNamara, similarly speaks to these dilemmas.

We rightly want future presidents to take reasonable risks and strive to serve all the people and not just those who bankrolled their candidacy. We want, as well, for presidents to have the intellectual courage to do what is right even when it is not popular or easy, and to instruct, inspire, and somehow transport us to a new and better place.

Finally, courage also involves having the guts not to give up after initial political and legislative defeats—yet like Lincoln, FDR, and other successful presidents, also have the pragmatic flexibility to accept occasional defeats and know when to move on to more important issues.

Ambition/Drive

Presidents need uncommon ambition and personal drive, yet not be so intoxicated with a need for power that they become unacceptably driven. Along with a lot of drive they also have to have a shrewd understanding and appreciation for the collaborative give-and-take of politics. Politics isn't beanbag. "It is dirty work in the engine-room (of state) but the ship would not move without it—or those prepared to undertake it," writes British journalist Henry Fairlie.[18]

Ambition, "fire in the belly," and even certain levels of ruthlessness are essential. The uncommon politician must be a person of physical and moral endurance. "Enjoyment of the game, ambition, ruthlessness, stamina, the ability to judge men and occasions: these may not seem to be lofty qualities to look for in the extraordinary politician, but they are, in fact, the reassuring ones. We should not in all this be too squeamish," writes Fairlie, in one of the best books on the life of politics.[19]

An often-told story about young Teddy Roosevelt nicely illustrates this point. Born to a privileged family, TR passed through Harvard College with high grades and a splendid network of other well-heeled, well-connected elites. Back home in New York he attended Columbia Law School and began to take a keen interest in local politics. His friends were chagrined. Politics, they sniffed, was "low," and beneath patrician ways. But such an attitude, Roosevelt wrote in his autobiography, "merely meant that the people I knew did not belong to the governing class and that the other people did—and that I intended to be one of the governing class; that if they proved too hard-bit for me I supposed I would have to quit."[20]

Roosevelt was short and plagued by asthma and poor vision, yet he personified pluck, stamina, and ambition. He relentlessly strengthened himself and, on a few occasions, seemed to enjoy punching people out. Roosevelt understood virtue in the human sense of the word: manliness. He prepared himself accordingly—as a big-game hunter and as a soldier. Even at Harvard, the young, self-conscious Roosevelt wrote that his classmates would "have had a tendency to look down upon me for doing Sunday School work [he taught Sunday School class] if I had not also been a corking boxer."[21]

Some people say it would be nice, occasionally at least, for a presidential candidate to look as though he or she was drafted rather than overtly hungering after the honor. Similarly it is sometimes noted, only half jokingly, that anyone who is so willing to submit himself to the incredibly exacting presidential nominating process must be borderline pathological, and thus may be mentally and perhaps morally unqualified for the job. The reality is that he or she who waits to be called to the presidency will wait and wait and wait. And those who have so much integrity or dignity that the brutal campaigning necessary to win is beneath them will never get invited. To get and serve in the presidency requires enormous ambition. We must learn to admire it—and work to see (through various checks and balances) that this personal ambition is contained within healthy limits.

Optimism

We love presidents who raise our hopes, remind us of our past triumphs, and persuade us it is "morning in America."

This optimism helped elect FDR over Hoover, Kennedy over Nixon, Reagan over Carter, and Bill Clinton over Bob Dole. Americans yearn for leaders to bring us together and bring out the best in us. We want them to challenge both themselves and ourselves to do better—and be better. Think of those who mounted the successful movements in America—abolitionists, progressives, women's rights activists, civil rights activists, environmentalists—all led efforts to liberate and free some aspect of American life and to extend the blessings of freedom to more and more people. Presidents rarely led any of these movements, yet they are expected to embrace them when they can (when the timing is right) and to enhance everyone's opportunity to achieve the American Dream.

"A president must hold out hope, must exude an optimism even in impossible circumstances," wrote *Time* magazine's Hugh Sidey. "History is a marvelous collection of stories about men and women who refused to accept the common verdict that certain achievements were impossible."[22]

FDR's "we have nothing to fear but fear itself" prescribed hope more than anything else in the darkest days of our depression. Susan Anthony, leader of the suffragette movement, simply proclaimed of her cause that "failure is impossible." To optimists politics is always the art of making possible tomorrow what appears impossible today, and politics is always an opportunity—never an obligation.

Nothing in the Constitution stipulates we have to elect a leader with a sunny disposition. And though we yearn for hope and inspiration we also want someone in the White House who will be a hardheaded realist. Yet, especially at election time, people want presidents who will use what Teddy Roosevelt called the "bully pulpit" to shed light on, and not darken, our prospects. "America didn't become great being pessimistic and cynical," Ronald Reagan liked to say, "America is built on a can-do spirit that sees every obstacle as a challenge, every problem as an opportunity."[23]

Thus, we want leaders who will cheer us on—and who will do so with an irresistible zest for life, a zest for challenges, a zest in the climb. The compelling transcendent moments in the history of America have been triumphs of a bullish or even irrational exuberance, a precedent set by the American Revolution.[24]

Strength and Toughness

We may talk a lot about wanting presidents to be sincere, honest, and ethical, yet we most assuredly want someone in the White House who will have the backbone to defend and preserve the nation—someone, if the times warrant it, who is willing "to bargain with the devil," be ruthless, and even to kill on our behalf.

Political theorist Niccolò Machiavelli minced no words when he advised that "a prince should have no other object, nor any thought, nor take anything else as his art but that of war and its orders and discipline."[25]

Playwright Arthur Miller described this as a central part of the star quality we yearn for, and that a great president, in common with a great actor, "must hold in himself an element of potential dangerousness."[26]

Nearly two-thirds of our presidents have served in the military, and ten were generals, including Washington, Jackson, Grant, and Eisenhower. Zachary Taylor is less well known because he died in his second year in office. "Old Rough and Ready" was his nickname, acquired because of his service in the War of 1812, in the Indian wars against the Black Hawks and Seminoles, and as the victorious military leader in the Mexican War.

We forgave Lincoln's constitutional violations during the Civil War and FDR's duplicity before we entered World War II, because we ultimately understand that every nation has its Machiavellian moments, and that the U.S. Constitution was never intended as a suicide pact. But exactly how do we smoke out of presidential candidates how they would act in these "mission-critical" moments? How do we distinguish between bombast and courage; how do we predict who might waver fatally and who can be trusted to act with appropriate caution? Will they be "rough and ready" only when the circumstances warrant action?

We fervently hope presidents can achieve our security through diplomatic initiatives. But we know this hasn't always been the case—nor will it. A president is now a permanent commander in chief of a permanently standing military. Presidents also preside over the intelligence agencies, the FBI, and the sprawling Department of Homeland Security. Hardly a week goes by when a president doesn't have to be "a decider" when it comes to arming the country, protecting its borders, and worrying about real and potential terrorist attacks. Most Americans gladly delegate these responsibilities to presidents and members of Congress.

But the lessons of Lincoln in the Civil War, Wilson in World War I, FDR in World War II, Truman with his atomic bomb decision at the close of that war, Kennedy in the Cuban Missile Crisis, and George W. Bush with his antiterrorist efforts remind us that a central part of the presidential job description is an understanding of our security interests and an appreciation of all the options in the event our security is seriously threatened.

Toughness or strength in a president also involves being able to say no to close friends and donors and being able to fire civilian and military advisers who are not doing their jobs. Truman fired General Douglas MacArthur, and it cost him popularity even though MacArthur's insubordination made it the right decision. Gerald Ford pardoned Richard Nixon, and though it may have been the right thing to do, it probably cost him his chances to be reelected.

Toughness involves having the discipline to say no, to stay focused, and to establish sensible priorities (for one's self and the nation) and then marshal all one's energies to fight for them.

Learner/Listener

We want presidents to welcome advice and to have intellectual curiosity and a profound sense of history and constitutionalism.

We know presidents will occasionally fail, as Kennedy did with the Bay of Pigs operation. But we also want them to able to admit error, as Kennedy did, and to learn from their failures. We want presidents who are relentless questioners and good listeners, who can squint with their ears and study, explore, discover, and bring out the best in other people—especially their advisers. The president as learner and teacher is also expected to help educate the public about the role of the federal government and about their own responsibilities as well as rights as citizens.

Presidents are necessarily generalists. But they have to recruit and learn from expert policy specialists in dozens of specialties from trade economists and genome scientists to China and Russia experts. A president is constantly dealing with complexity and uncertainties. Former presidents and their advisers regularly write in their memoirs that in almost every national security crisis there was never enough information available at the time action was required. Robert McNamara's remembrances in the film *The Fog of War* repeatedly make this point.

Presidents have to have the disciplined toughness to learn whether or not they should act, when to wait, when to commit forces, and when to demand yet more persuasive evidence. Should FDR have been better prepared for Pearl Harbor? Was Truman right to drop the atomic bomb on Japan? Were JFK and LBJ right to escalate troop forces in Vietnam? Was Clinton wrong in not coming to aid those massacred in Rwanda? Was George W. Bush right or wrong to invade Iraq as he did? These are tough questions—heatedly debated to this day—about presidential discipline and the extent to which presidents educate themselves about contemporary issues and draw appropriate conclusions.

One more note on learning: We want, and indeed should insist, that a future president have a strong understanding of U.S. and world history and constitutionalism. He or she needs, as well, to have a sophisticated grasp of how governments and markets work, and how trade and diplomacy work. Necessary, too, is a thoughtful respect and understanding for the diverse political cultures in the United States.

In sum, listening, learning, and teaching skills are essential. A leader has to both listen to and lead us and constantly remember that leadership is all about achieving mutually shared aspirations. We want presidents who give us a sense not only of who they are, but more important, of who we are and what we as a nation might become.

Self-Confidence and Humility

We want presidents who have a healthy sense of who they are, their strengths and weaknesses.

Much has been written in recent years about social and emotional intelligence—the ability to relate to people, to have a positive outlook in the social dynamics that are central to complex organizations. "Comfortable in his or her own skin" is a modern-day cliché used to describe leaders in professional life. Like most clichés it is rather simplistic, yet it is also in part suggestive. For we want someone in the White House who has a robust level of self-confidence and knows how to instill confidence in his or her team. In the shadow of Richard Nixon, Jimmy Carter, and George W. Bush, we justifiably look at future candidates through an almost psychological lens—searching for signs of any insecurities, malice, malaise, or rigidity that may lurk beneath their coached appearances of warmth and likeability.

Self-confidence developed too far leads to arrogance or narcissism. Most leaders must be somewhat egotistical or even narcissistic. They have to believe they can make a difference. They have to believe in their abilities to listen, learn, and execute. But as in the Greek fable about Narcissus, self-love carried too far becomes self-intoxicating and can be fatal. Here again we confront one of the great paradoxes of leadership: Too much self-confidence breeds arrogance. We may want humility in our leaders, yet excessive humility can be just as paralyzing as excessive self-confidence.

Thus we want leaders with optimism about self, about life, and about opportunities for organizational and societal breakthroughs. Indeed, we want leaders with fearlessness and contagious self-confidence. But "beware the presidential contender who lacks emotional intelligence," writes political scientist Fred Greenstein. "In its absence all else may turn to ashes."[27] For the qualities of a good leader must include empathy, curiosity, and humility.

Humility involves thinking about yourself less, not thinking less of yourself. The emotionally balanced leader understands this principle and has a balanced sense of self-awareness, self-confidence, and humility that earns respect and trust and grants him or her the leeway to govern. Here again, Lincoln and Washington serve as sensible role models. In short, we want tenacity and discipline balanced with humility. Self-confidence and self-esteem as well as thick skin help in this generally thankless assignment. The ability to laugh at oneself and admit one's errors are similarly crucial.

Not wanted are politicians who are rigid, defensive, and torn by self-pity and self-doubt, or who are less guided by public-spirited visions than by personal needs to settle scores and get elected, or who blame their problems on the media and are prone to punish people on their personal "enemies' lists."

Understanding and Liking People

This final personal attribute we want in presidents may sound obvious. Still, it deserves emphasis: We want presidents to like and enjoy interacting with people—people from all classes and all walks of life. Even though we want presidents to be better than we are, we also want them to be like us in the sense that they understand and can represent us.

Much is made of the myth of the common man in American life. And this endures in part because we yearn to have everyone's situation taken into account. We want presidents, then, to understand that everyone goes through peaks and valleys, everyone is subject to risks, family adversity, and personal setbacks. We want presidents who have shared in these common experiences—who can convey a "you are not alone" and "I feel your pain" attitude. FDR had this, and Bill Clinton made it a central part of his campaign leadership style.

Someone once suggested that one appropriate test for presidential candidates is to have them, sequentially, spend a morning with first or second graders as a substitute teacher. How would they do? Could their love of people be demonstrated with unaffiliated and apolitical youngsters? And how would children respond to the candidates as people? We want, in short, for candidates to prove that their rapport with others is more than contrived.

I turn now to what are the most important *political skills* we should want in leading presidential candidates.

Political Savvy

Many people mistakenly yearn for candidates who are apolitical or somehow above politics. But you can't take the politics out of the presidency any more than you can take the presidency out of politics.

It is an enormously political job, and a president has to be a skilled, astute political operative. Presidents need to understand the necessity for politics and welcome the political pulling and tugging and the inevitable political conflict that comes with the job. Presidents need to welcome working regularly with people of all political views and to appreciate that bargaining, negotiating, and agreement-making are a central and constant part of the job. "He or she knows how to cut a deal." That may sound somehow ignoble—yet it is at the heart of politics.

We like our presidential candidates to have strong, consistent principles and to speak as freely as possible in absolutes where things are defined as black or white. "Yet there is no core principle or set of principles shared by all Americans," writes former presidential candidate and U.S. senator Orrin Hatch. "A politician can't help but violate some voters' principles because no constituency is monolithic."[28]

Here is how Liberia's president, Ellen Johnson-Sirleaf (Africa's first female head of state), discusses conviction and compromise. "Compromise is politics. No matter how strong you are in your convictions, no matter how courageous in your actions," she says, "at some point compromises are necessary along the way to accommodate the views and the feelings of others without necessarily undermining in any meaningful way the things you believe and the principles for which you stand." She adds, "If you're too inflexible, then of course all your good intentions could be totally disrupted or undermined."[29]

One of the arts of politics is knowing when to hold firm and when to strike a deal. It's usually a matter of timing and often a question of what is achievable. Take the example of the right amount for the minimum wage. There are always political groups wanting it raised. Likewise there are always those who want no, or merely a bare minimum, increase. The question usually boils down—every ten years or so when this issue arises—to whether to press your principled view and not compromise or to compromise at some imperfect yet achievable halfway measure. It rarely comes down to an all-or-nothing resolution.[30]

Political savvy involves defining issues and knowing which issues to embrace and which to defer to another day. Political savvy also involves a sensitivity to public opinion and knowing when to play a critical role either in accepting majority thinking or trying to rally public opinion behind an issue with all the educating and persuading this involves. Mayor Frank Skeffington in the classic political film *The Last Hurrah* (1958) says the trick in politics is not only knowing what the people want, but "what they will settle for" and how to negotiate the compromises toward that end.

Politically savvy presidential candidates learn to talk in broad, general terms about possible new policy directions. They know they need to be both programmatic and pragmatic. They may have to veer right or left to win their party's nomination, yet they understand the old aphorism that the only extreme that usually wins in American elections is the extreme middle. They understand too that they are not running for the position of national political philosopher. Thus, their linkage of ends and means and their hierarchy of priorities are often hazy.

FDR told his aides that a presidential election was less a time for adult education than it was a time for winning votes and getting elected. He would, he said, first win the office and later—after he had won—work on educating the public. FDR, writes James MacGregor Burns, borrowed heavily from Jefferson and Teddy Roosevelt. He would embrace liberty and repudiate privilege, yet skip back and forth across the ideological spectrum. It was "a broad canvas on which he could fill in his own shifting views and values, depending on election needs," write Burns and Dunn. "But it also drained his political philosophy of vigor and structure. . . . It was not that FDR had no ideology in the early 1930s but that his doctrinal array was so soft and shapeless, so malleable in its central organization, as to become a frail edifice of related and unrelated ends and means."[31] This harsh yet accurate description could equally describe much of the political philosophy, or lack thereof, of winning candidates such as JFK, Jimmy Carter, and Bill Clinton—all of whom lived politically in FDR's long shadow.

Political savvy, especially at the candidate stage, plainly involves fund-raising—the ability to get people to invest in your candidacy so as to guarantee that your ideas, issues, and promises will get a fair hearing. Occasionally candidates at all levels of politics are indifferent or even condescending about the need to raise money for their candidacies. Such a view reflects a lack of political savvy. To be taken seriously in American politics—at least the way our election system is arranged—candidates must market themselves and their ideas. This is just one of the political realities, degrading though fund-raising may be, a serious modern candidate has to accept.

Strategic Thinker

Public policymaking involves calculating the costs and consequences of national decisions. We want presidents to have the ability to clarify the key issues of the day, get all the pertinent data, understand the probabilities, define what is achievable, and set sensible priorities for what should be done.

Presidents and their advisers will be held accountable when they fail to understand the ramifications of federal initiatives or the lack thereof. Bush's decision to invade Iraq with inadequate understanding of what was required to secure that nation came back to haunt him as well as the country. Similarly, the failure of several administrations to help prevent the devastation of Hurricane Katrina or genocidal civil wars in Africa also haunts presidents and all of us.

Presidents need to surround themselves with strategic thinkers in all the top policy fields. They need to know how to reach out and commission long-range studies on hundreds of topics ranging from U.S.-Russian relations to how best to upgrade science and engineering education in America.

Presidents constantly must ask the tough "what if" counterfactual questions. What if the nation's largest hedge funds implode? What if there are a dozen Katrina disasters? What if virtually all manufacturing gets exported? What if Israel gets attacked by a coalition of Iran, Syria, and their allies?

We may elect generalists to the presidency, yet we want them, unfairly or not, to become leading experts and supervise the nation's leading experts on hundreds of complex policy issues. And they have to be mindful of the political bias all their advisers bring to the table and the distortions brought about by inevitable bureaucratic in-fighting.[32]

A president is asked to focus on all the large, compelling policy challenges of the day—and to do so in an unsentimental, strategic way. He or she is asked to be a forest person, transcending the trees and the leaves; more hedgehog than fox; more wholesaler than retailer; more leader than manager, able to establish priorities and then to fight for them.

Coalition Builder

To govern is to build coalitions, form alliances, and orchestrate agreements, all in an effort to achieve mutually shared goals.

Getting elected requires candidates to pull together an electoral coalition. Governing requires the development of numerous coalitions, one for at least every plank in a candidate's platform. We must ask of presidential candidates how capable they are in mobilizing groups and factions and how effective they are in bringing them together to work toward solving mutual problems. How have they done in the past and with what success? How are they doing in their campaigns?

We want presidents to be skilled social architects with the ability to weave together diverse groups in order to overcome the natural fragmentation in our highly decentralized society. This means understanding conflict and understanding that conflict is inevitable. Conflict will always exist in a society that believes, as Americans do, in liberty and capitalism.

Marx and Madison both wrote that there will be factions if there is an unequal distribution of property. And that is the case. The rich and the poor, to simplify complexity, will regularly divide on issues such as taxes, welfare benefits, minimum wage levels, and the like. Ideology, religion, nationalism, and contending views about the proper role of government similarly divide us into factionalism.

Presidents as coalition builders not only have to understand what makes people think politically, they also have to devise ways for people to achieve common ground. That is the central challenge of governing in a democratic society. How good will this candidate be as a negotiator? How good as a bargainer? What talent does he or she have in getting people to compromise so as to advance common interests—and the national interest?

Morale Builder

The presidency is far more than just a political or managerial job. It is also an institution and office that has to help Americans through valleys as well as over peaks, through crises and transitions. Presidents must help unify us when we experience tragedy and setbacks.

Presidents at their best help remind us of our mutual obligations, shared values, and the trust and caring that can hold us together in our responsibilities to one another. Americans yearn for national leaders who will be uniters not dividers, who can both bring us together and challenge us—and the country as a whole—to be better.

George Washington understood this role. He was one of the few continental figures of his day, and his integrity, judgment, and service to his nation were cherished. He appreciated that a living, real Constitution includes customs, traditions, practices, and precedent-setting leadership to fill out the vagueness of the written Constitution. As a man uncommonly devoted to the Roman ideal of civic virtue, he made his own interests subservient to those of the nation and thus became a remarkable unifying figure, a warrior-hero and symbol-in-chief for the new nation.

Lincoln's performance also left an indelible mark on the presidency. In his uncanny ability to be a common man with uncommon instincts he presided over our most trying calamity and encouraged a rebirth and liberation the nation urgently needed.

Political scientist Clinton Rossiter overstates it, yet calls Lincoln the supreme American icon, the richest symbol in our culture. "He is," wrote Rossiter, "the martyred Christ of democracy's passion play. And who then can measure the strength that is given to the President because he holds Lincoln's office, lives in Lincoln's house, and walks in Lincoln's way?"[33] The Lincoln story is profound in meaning and symbol—and it makes it hard on those who follow in his footsteps—in part because the myth and majesty of his performance continue to grow in reputation. But the Lincoln lesson is this: He appealed to our better angels and helped his nation renew its commitment to liberty and justice for all. He unlocked the higher aspirations and promise of America. By his example, each successive generation has sought leadership of comparable promise.

FDR, JFK, Reagan, and Bill Clinton understood this Washington-Lincoln legacy of morale building. They understood that rituals, pageants, and symbolic leadership were part of the job. They knew the need for a president to reaffirm our basic goals, celebrate freedom, and participate in rituals that help people understand the larger events of which they are a part.

When we judge presidential candidates, then, we need to ask if they fully understand this additional part of the job and whether they have what it takes to perform these civil religious responsibilities.

Persuasive Communicator

Ideas and wisdom are of little use if a president cannot rally the Congress, his or her party, and the public around key priorities and initiatives.

A president has to be an effective motivator. Speaking, debating, and television presentation skills are crucial. There is an old saying that if people cannot communicate well, they probably can't think well, and if this is so, others will do their thinking for them. Politics is one long conversation or debate about how best to govern and by what principles. Presidents are rightly expected to define, defend, and convincingly argue their point of view. They need substance in what they say, yet they also need voice, power, and persuasive projection in their delivery.

Presidential politics involves an enormous amount of advocacy, debate, and public presentation. Modern presidential campaigns, despite all their flaws, allow for plenty of opportunities to judge a candidate's persuasiveness. But the persuasive demands of the presidential job are vastly greater still than the job of campaigning for the office. For in office a president must rally many constituencies, ranging from his or her own cabinet, to the whole nation, and, very often, world leaders and world opinion as well.

Consider the following as part of the job specs: inaugural address, state of the union address, White House press briefings, summit meeting talks, legislative leader deliberations, addresses to hundreds of business and professional associations, motivational talks to government employees, talks to the nation after national tragedies, eulogies at funerals, talks to religious leaders, interviews with leading reporters and on television talk shows—and countless related appearances or "performances." Everything a president says is instantly analyzed for its political meaning, political impact, and authenticity.

Stagecraft Performance Skills

We understandably tire of candidates or presidents who substitute sound bites for substance. And we don't want political leaders who become overly preoccupied with the ceremonial or symbolic aspects of their job (even though, as described above, those too are certainly a part of the job).

Still, effective presidents have a lot in common with effective actors.[34] They have to listen to and read their audiences. They have to know when to talk and when to listen. Presidents have to have the stamina of TR, the humility and vulnerability of Lincoln, the dramatic flare of FDR, the wit of JFK, the communication skills of Ronald Reagan, and the zest for politics that Bill Clinton has had. Then too, of course, we ask them to be themselves.

Presidents learn to develop the art of acting—not because it is in the Constitution's Article II that outlines presidential power and not because we recruit actors or actresses, but because we live in an age of entertainment/information and presidents are thrust onto a stage with a national audience of 320-plus million, not to mention vast overseas international audiences. We ask them not to lie to us. But we insist they tell us their story, and our story, and that they inspire us so we can make progress on all the noble ends outlined in the Constitution's preamble.

Stagecraft skills are invaluable political skills. It is easy to ridicule some of them, yet a would-be president who is deficient in those matters is handicapped. (Hoover and Carter come to mind, as well as candidates Mondale, Dukakis, Bradley, and Kerry). Novelist Umberto Eco compared two of Italy's top politicians this way: "Berlusconi has the advantage of being a big actor. Prodi is not an actor, which is not a crime, but it is a weakness."[35] Prodi's tenure was brief. Berlusconi returned in 2008 for a "second act."

The legendary British actor Sir Laurence Olivier noted that an actor might occasionally have a small audience, yet he can never give a small performance. Likewise with presidents—they are constantly on stage with entrances and exits every day all year, sometimes with small though usually with large, demanding audiences, and always with the expectation, fair or not, of splendid performances rich in substance and rich with dignity.

Political leaders, like actors and playwrights, need at times to get people to transcend their cynicism, grief, and despair and pull together for the common good. Actors and playwrights get people to suspend their disbelief. Politicians, in like manner, have to convince people that these are no ordinary times. We are no ordinary people—and ultimately we will prevail.

FDR, Reagan, Bill Clinton, and Barack Obama have all been actors in the sense that they have been skilled storytellers, masters at self-presentation and in projecting empathy and relaxed sincerity. They came alive and sometimes even glowed when on the national stage.

Politics is, and always has been, part theater. To govern requires leaders to learn how to act, read, rally, and connect with large audiences. No degree of institutionalized bureaucracy can ever replace the need for charismatic leadership. The capacity to inspire is the difference separating the leader from a manager or bureaucrat.

Executive Competence

Leaders are people, as discussed earlier, who figure out what is needed, and what is right, and know how to mobilize both people and resources to achieve mutually shared goals.

Leadership involves many things—intuition, inspiration, and coalition and morale building—yet it is also part managerial or administrative. National leaders, especially a president, have to have the ability to recruit extraordinary advisers and administrators. They need, too, the wisdom to delegate to teams of colleagues. We want evidence of experience and competence in bringing people together in teams to solve major policy problems. This was painfully absent, for example, in the U.S. response to the Gulf Coast Katrina disaster and to postoccupation efforts in Iraq.

Doris Kearns Goodwin's *Team of Rivals* (2005) celebrates how Abraham Lincoln, who had virtually no administrative experience, cleverly recruited his three chief rivals from the 1860 Republican nominating competition. He did so because, unlike himself, they had executive experience and because, as he emphasized at the time, the crisis the country was facing could only be rectified by the best available talent.[36]

Presidents as executives have to be good at firing their colleagues up or else firing them off. No politician likes to fire people. Presidents too often fail to fire incompetent administrators when they first begin to have their doubts about them. One of the chief lessons from both government and business is that when people deserve to be fired it should be done as soon as possible. Delaying it causes problems for everyone. Too much executive branch time is spent dealing with mistakes made at the recruiting stage. Getting the right people on the bus and getting the wrong people off the bus are fundamental in any healthy organization.[37]

We recruit politicians, as opposed to administrative geniuses, to the White House. Yet we judge presidents every day on how well (or not so well) they are running the federal government and its major bureaucracies. Presidents may lack the skill or interest to manage effectively, but they neglect managerial responsibilities at considerable risk. Inattention to personnel matters and policy implementation often causes critical problems. Indeed, many of the mistakes and serious blunders of recent presidential administrations can be traced directly to inadequate attention paid to the administrative responsibilities that are a central part of being president. (Bay of Pigs, Iran-Contra, Katrina, Iraq—to name just a few).

Practice, Not Perfection

No presidential candidate scores a perfect "A" on all of these qualities and skills. And no prospective president is ever fully prepared for a Civil War, 1929, Pearl Harbor, Cuban Missile Crisis, 9/11 attacks, and similar exacting challenges. What we pragmatically look for is to see who has the best combination of these assets and then compare and contrast from among the viable rivals.

Do we ask too much of our presidential candidates? Sure we do. History conditions different cultures to expect different things of their leaders. In the United States we exaggerate the capacity for what even heroic presidents have done to shape the course of events. Presidents live in a world in which perfection is the aspiration, but deal making, self-promotion, and compromise are regularly necessary.[38] As pointed out, however, we aren't likely to lower our expectations. Talented politicians are indispensable to making our constitutional democracy work.

Three cheers for those who run, and for all their helpers and advisers who provide us choices. Americans will never be satisfied with our candidates, nor should we be. The ideal or perfect presidential candidate is probably a fictional entity, for the dream candidate would be able to please everyone and make conflict disappear.

But our love of liberty invites diversity and therefore disagreements of ideology and values. Politicians and presidential candidates as well as the people they represent have different ideas about what is best for the nation. That's why we have politics, candidates, debates, and elections.

To hope for a society without conflict, and thus without politics and politicians, is to hope for a utopia that will never be realized.

Chapter Two
The Symbolic and Shamanistic Functions of the American Presidency

> It is no exaggeration to say that all modern political prose descends from [Lincoln's] Gettysburg Address. . . . In his brief time before the crowd at Gettysburg he wove a spell that has not, yet, been broken—he called up a new nation out of the blood and trauma.
>
> —Garry Wills[1]

The American presidency is more than a political or constitutional institution. It is a focus for intense emotions. The presidency serves our basic need for a visible and representative national symbol to which we can turn with hopes and aspirations.

Presidents are the nation's number one celebrity; almost everything they do is news. Merely by going to a sports event, a funeral, a celebration of a national holiday, or by visiting another country, presidents not only command attention, they convey meaning. By their actions presidents can arouse a sense of honor or dishonor, hope or despair.

Although Americans like to view themselves as hard-headed pragmatists, they—like humans everywhere—cannot stand too much reality. Man does not live by reason alone. Myth and dreams are age-old forms of escape. And people turn to national leaders just as tribesmen turn to shamans—yearning for meaning, healing, empowerment, legitimacy, assurance, patriotism, and a sense of purpose.

Americans expect many things from their presidents—honesty, credibility, crisis leadership, agenda-setting and administrative abilities, as well as certain of the tribal leader or priestly functions we usually associate with primitive or religious communities. A president's personal conduct affects how millions of Americans view their political loyalties and civic responsibilities. Of course, the symbolic influence of presidents is not always evoked in favor of worthy causes, and sometimes presidents do not live up to our expectations of moral leadership. Still, a great many people find comfort in an oversimplified image of presidents as warrior-captains firmly at the helm of the ship of state, as emancipators or liberators in the exodus tradition, as priests and prophets of our civil religion, and as defenders of the democratic faith and evocative spokesmen of the American Dream.

United in this one institution are multiple roles that are on the surface confusing and conflicting. A president's unifying role as a head of state and symbol-in-chief, especially in times of crisis, often clashes with his or her advocacy of program initiatives and partisan responsibilities, including as the de facto head of his or her party. Further, presidents invariably take advantage of and borrow from their legitimacy as representative and symbolic heads of state to expand their political and partisan influence.

The framers of the U.S. Constitution did not fully anticipate the symbolic and morale-building functions a president would have to perform. Certain magisterial functions such as receiving ambassadors and granting pardons were conferred. In fact, the job of the presidency demanded symbolic leadership from the beginning. Washington and his advisers would readily recognize that in leadership at its finest, the leader symbolizes the best in the community, the best in its traditions, values, and purposes. Effective leadership infuses vision and a sense of significance into the enterprise of a nation.

The Importance of George Washington

The American Constitution, as drafted and ratified in the late 1780s, was a splendid document. Yet it did not guarantee that the American presidency would work and that Americans would enjoy both representative and effective government. Much depended on how George Washington interpreted the Constitution and how his countrymen would respond to his leadership. He carefully would have to lessen the distrust of Americans to a centralized leadership institution and earn respect and legitimacy for the fledgling Republic.

George Washington was one of the few continental figures of his day. He was already a warrior-hero. He had commanded with distinction the revolutionary patriots for an eight-year period. In victory he became a prime symbol of triumph. His integrity, judgment, and lengthy service (both in and out of uniform) to his country and his devotion to his troops and his countrymen set him apart from his fellow founders.

Washington wasn't a great philosopher, orator, lawyer, or even organizer. Even his military abilities have been questioned. His mind was keen, yet not especially inventive or imaginative. Yet the nation needed a hero. America had had no heritage of celebrated public servants, other than those in England, and hence it was essential for national pride to endow our first hero with lavish praise. His countrymen did precisely this. And Washington understood their need and not only accepted it graciously, he used it as a means of legitimizing both his new office and the new national government he had labored so long to bring into being.

No matter how ably others had explained the Constitution, and especially the provisions for presidential leadership, it was now up to President Washington to carry out the promise of the office and establish the precedents to be followed as long as the country survived. Washington was fully aware that the process of making the Constitution work had only just begun. He knew that written documents do not implement themselves. He appreciated that a living, real constitution includes customs, traditions, practices, interpretations, and precedent setting to fill out the vagueness of the written provisions.

Among President Washington's many legacies to our political system was his acting out superbly the head-of-state and symbolic functions we now regularly expect of presidents. When the founders decided to grant the chief executive the additional responsibilities of receiving ambassadors and other foreign dignitaries, they in effect made the president head of state and chief symbolic leader as well. Our constitutional framers devoted little thought to these head-of-state obligations. It was one of the many unfinished aspects of their work.

The framers may not have spelled out the symbolic roles of the presidency for two reasons. First, they yearned to devise a system that was a government of laws rather than a government that depended on indispensable individuals. More than anything they were trying to invent new forms of government and constitutionalism that moved away from the British model. On the other hand, the availability of Washington and the expectation that he would serve as the first president doubtless had much to do with their leaving these aspects of the presidency underdefined. For in Washington they realized they had a person not only of commanding presence but also of considerable optimism, vision, and devotion to civic duty.[2] Washington interpreted his new position as having important, semiroyal responsibilities. He would travel throughout the nation as a symbol of the new government. He would appear with the American troops to lend morale and legitimacy to their missions. He would demand respect from the officers in both the executive and legislative departments of government. In short, he was ever sensitive to the reality that he was expected to be far more than a national city manager. He had to symbolize both the past glories and the future greatness of his new nation. He had, in addition, to win respect and establish credibility and even a certain amount of mystique in this new institution called the American presidency.

In certain ways Washington became the nation's first secular priest or societal shaman. In helping his fellow countrymen to transcend their parochial loyalties he helped instill a new nationalism and a new sense of collective purpose. His combination of *warrior* and *priest, liberator,* and *definer* of a national vision presaged additional extraconstitutional responsibilities for future American presidents.

The Warrior Symbol

In deciding to make the executive office also the place for commander-in-chief responsibilities, the framers fused together the roles of executive leadership and military or security leadership. This unification, which had been absent under the Articles of Confederation and especially during the American Revolution, guaranteed that Americans would expect presidents to know about war, be capable of wartime leadership, and, if possible, have military experience. Not surprisingly, then, we have elected several military heroes. Washington, Jackson, Grant, and Eisenhower were elected in this spirit.

Americans honor their heroes and want presidents to be heroic at the same time they want them to be representative. They have always revered the explorer and risk-taking entrepreneur. Thus Christopher Columbus, Charles Lindbergh, and John Glenn were all put on a pedestal. So also were presidents who had demonstrated valor in service to their country.

Washington, Jackson, Grant, Teddy Roosevelt, and Eisenhower all benefited from their military achievements, and these enhanced their legitimacy as presidential candidates. And the presidency itself—because of these warrior-presidents—took on additional meaning because of their presence. Each brought to the office some of the aura of legend and the charisma of reputation and authority earned in defense of the nation-state. This never guaranteed effectiveness in presidential performance, something it quite notably did not do for Grant, yet it expanded the public's acceptance of their authority—and in four of their cases it helped achieve for them rather high evaluations for their presidencies.

Part of the symbolic responsibility of the American president is to preside over the cultural and ritual observances of the nation. Memorial and Veteran's Day ceremonies are prime illustrations. So also are the centennials and anniversaries of the conclusions of past wars. Then, too, the modern president is required to assure the nation of its military strength.

George Washington's personal leadership in helping to end the Whiskey Rebellion in 1793 and Dwight Eisenhower's famous pledge, "I shall go to Korea," are examples of personalized presidential military leadership. The legend of Jackson and his victory at New Orleans, of Grant and his military effectiveness in ending the Civil War, and of Teddy Roosevelt and his Rough Riders at San Juan all add to the memory and cumulative symbolic legacy of the presidency at large. TR's pugnacious temperament as a glory-seeking president in the buildup of naval power and in the building of the Panama Canal also reinforced his exuberant and expansive use of presidential power.

Military heroes rise to leadership roles in every society, and ours is no exception. To their credit, military leaders who have become presidents have bent over backwards not to unnecessarily militarize the presidency. Yet the emergence of the nation as the leading military power in the world necessarily blurs the distinction between the dual roles of the president as head of government and commander in chief. Once merely one of the jobs of the president and only an occasionally demanding aspect of the job, the modern president is compelled to spend at least half of his or her time planning national security strategy and presiding over a sprawling military complex, often with as many as 500,000 troops in uniform stationed at several hundred bases in nearly 60 nations.

The Emancipator-Liberator Symbol

The Exodus or emancipator theory of emergency leadership is now deeply embedded in the cultural consciousness of the West. The Exodus is an account of deliverance or liberation both in religious and secular terms. The Exodus paradigm is one of liberation, of a march to freedom. Just as the Exodus for the Israelites was a journey forward, a march to a goal, a moral progress, so also in their own way Americans have had to march against forces of despotism and oppression. Invariably, they have relied upon uncommon leadership for this purpose.

The American Revolution itself, although in many ways a conservative revolution, was a war of liberation and a determined striving to bring about deliverance. If an aspiration or hope motivated that rebellion, forceful and committed leadership was needed to help realize the triumph. The legend of George Washington is inextricably linked to this, Americans' own story of liberation.

Yet it is Abraham Lincoln who epitomizes the liberator-emancipator role of the American political leader. Lincoln's special role in American civic life comes not from his revelation of God's will, but because he revealed the higher truth latent in the Declaration of Independence that no man shall suffer in the bonds of slavery. With an eloquence second to no president in history, Lincoln articulated a vision of America, similar to Jefferson's, that has become an eternally lit beacon in our national memory.

Even a free people need their heroes, and it is our fortune that our foremost heroes have been those who by empowering us helped us transcend our flaws. If the real Lincoln was not exactly a saintly Emancipator, neither was he a racist. He grew as he rose to power and he grew also once he attained power. The flawed, fatalistic, and politically ambitious Lincoln struggled with himself, and in doing so helped his country struggle to resolve the haunting moral paradox of slavery in a nation based in the spirit of the Declaration of Independence. Ultimately, Lincoln provided transcending liberating leadership. Thus in late 1862 he would remind the Congress and the nation that the dogmas of the quiet past are inadequate to the stormy present. "The occasion is piled high with difficulty, and we must rise with the occasion. As our case is new, so we must think anew, and act anew. We must disenthrall ourselves, and then we shall save our country." "Fellow-citizens," Lincoln went on, "*we* cannot escape history. . . . The fiery trial through which we pass, will light us down, in honor or dishonor, to the latest generation. . . . In *giving* freedom to the *slave*, we *assure* freedom to the *free*—honorable alike in what we give, and what we preserve. We shall nobly save, or meanly lose, the last best, hope of earth."[3]

Lincoln, caught up in the turbulent social forces of his time, helped resolve one of the nation's most perplexing moral problems. The Lincoln myth is not that he was a political saint, but rather that he helped prod his countrymen toward redemption. In his actions, and even more in the legends that developed around him after his death, the Lincoln story is rich in meaning and symbol. It adds considerably to the legitimacy of the presidency and greatly expanded the public's expectations of the possibilities of presidential moral leadership. His failed predecessor, James Buchanan, and failed successor, Andrew Johnson, demonstrate by contrast the dismal effects of inept leadership.

Eighty years later, Franklin Roosevelt's determined personal leadership designed to cope with the devastation of the Great Depression also fit the emancipator-liberator symbolic role. Again, the legend and myths developed, often enlarged out of proportion. Yet in politics, the perception is usually as important and more lasting than the reality. Nowadays Roosevelt is remembered for his willingness to risk his political career to stake out bold new measures needed to rescue the nation from its worst economic disaster.

Through all his New Deal years, FDR recognized the nation needed renewal and hope. His "We have nothing to fear but fear itself" statement, his reassuring fireside chats, his contagious self-confidence and his often unwarranted optimism telegraphed to the American people that things would improve. This so-called traitor to his class would cast his lot with the common people. He would institute safeguards against speculators in the marketplace, he would put people to work on public projects, and he would introduce Social Security and enact countless other measures to spur economic recovery. And for all this FDR would become idolized by the working classes as a savior, as a renewer of the system, as a liberating leader.

Similarly, his risking all to come to the aid of the Allies in defeating fascism is also interpreted as leadership of liberation. Somehow, whether during the aftershocks of Pearl Harbor, the invasion of Normandy, or his personal diplomacy and visits to the troops in North Africa, Roosevelt seemed to be engaged in bringing new meaning to America's "Manifest Destiny." Although a wide variety of meanings were doubtless conveyed, the emancipator-liberator, the leader in defense of freedom, always loomed large and forms the FDR legends today: "a soldier of freedom," as his biographer James MacGregor Burns puts it, and, we might add, foremost architect as well of the modern American presidency.

Presidents as Defenders of the Faith

Every four years Americans elect a politician to serve as president. Yet we also yearn for a high priest of sorts, because despite our separation of church and state, we need performed for us some of the same functions that shamans, medicine men, and other practitioners of ritualistic arts perform in other societies.

From Jefferson to our day, presidents have personalized the job and helped remind Americans of the promise of our

Republic. Each president is asked, in some way, to help remind us of the greatness of our past and shape the course of a more exalted future.

Jefferson's inaugural addresses illustrate the singular nature of the role. His constant reiteration of his belief in the Democratic Faith is similarly illustrative of this tradition.

Woodrow Wilson's conception of the presidency was plainly in the Jeffersonian mold. His moral exhortations and optimism in a more assertive role for the national government and his idealistic faith in the promise of a League of Nations underscored his notions of a president as decidedly more than a mere administrator. Wilson often acted as if he were a prime minister or priest as he went about setting moral standards by which to guide both national and international behavior.[4] Wilson came to office with a capacious view of presidential leadership:

> His is the only national voice in affairs. Let him once win the admiration and confidence of the country, and no other single force can withstand him, no combination of force will easily overpower him. His position takes the imagination of the country. He is the representative of no constituency, but of the whole people.
>
> He may be both the leader of his party and the leader of the nation, or he may be one or the other. If he leads the nation, his party can hardly resist him. His office is anything he has the sagacity and force to make it.
>
> Some of our presidents have deliberately held themselves off from using the full power they might legitimately have used, because of conscientious scruples. . . . The President is at liberty, both in law and conscience, to be as big a man as he can.
>
> His is the vital place of action in the system, whether he accepts it as such or not, and the office is the measure of the man—of his measure as well as of his force.[5]

President John F. Kennedy also fits the defender of the faith and the renewer of the dream symbols closely associated with the symbolic presidency. In part, it was his glamour, style, youth, and wit. Yet it was also the Kennedy message of hope and the promise of new possibilities. He viewed America as having a special mission. He kept insisting that to say one is an American is a proud boast and that we had a lot to do to live up to that claim. "We can do better" was his campaign mantra. He liked to stress that this country "cannot afford to be materially rich and spiritually poor." We needed, he said, to complete the unredeemed pledges of the Roosevelt-Truman period, and we similarly needed to reclaim our political and military dominance in world affairs. His Peace Corps, man-to-the-moon program, overseas economic development initiatives, belated but significant civil rights action, and similar endeavors were intended to recapture the spirit and idealism of distinctive aspects of the American Dream.

In death the Kennedy legend is enlarged many times over, and we remember him less for what he did than for what he symbolized, what he began, what he talked about, and for the promise of what might have been. Although historians and political appraisers evaluate Kennedy as merely an average, or perhaps above-average, president, the American people remember Kennedy in a different and more reverential way. They remember the self-confidence, the optimism, the enthusiasm, the idealism, and the visions he shared.

It is one of the paradoxes or ironies of the Kennedy presidency that although he often lacked passion and moral commitment in a clear intellectual way—and he was most assuredly not a Churchill or an FDR—his personal impact on millions of Americans and others around the world was of a transcending kind, and his words, hopes, and personal example for a time helped lift people up from the everyday mundane realities that otherwise faced them. (For more on the Kennedy case, see Chapter 4.)

The Reagan presidency was plainly also rich with symbolism and meaning for many Americans. Reagan came to the White House promising a new American Dream—a dream that spoke of more freedom from government, lowered taxes, and less regulation of the entrepreneurial impulses of the nation. Reagan's definition of the American Dream differed in many ways from Roosevelt's, yet like Roosevelt, Reagan's initiatives often polarized the nation. In common with Roosevelt, Reagan received unusual public support and won an impressive reelection, perhaps in part because he was willing to take a stand, willing to defend his version of the American mission. If Reagan's was more of an act of restoration or redirection than an act of rebirth or liberation, some of Reagan's more ardent supporters view his role as very much as significant as the visionary, transcending leadership of a Lincoln and a Roosevelt.

Reagan had an uncanny understanding of the symbolic roles a capable president must perform. He had a conscious appreciation of the need for the president to reaffirm our basic goals, to celebrate liberty and freedom, and to participate fully in the rituals that both give meaning to American life and help people understand the larger events of which they are a minor part. Few presidents have been better than Reagan at helping the nation observe its rituals such as Memorial Day, the Fourth of July, Thanksgiving, Veteran's Day, our participation in the Olympics, summit diplomacy, and similar ceremonies. No one was better at performing national chaplain services—as Reagan did in comforting Americans after the *Challenger* disaster, or as he grieved with and gave meaning to those who mourned the tragic deaths of U.S. Marines in Lebanon, or the army troops downed in a transport crash in Canada as they returned from the Sinai. Reagan understood that Americans have a civil religion with semisacred symbols and that these reflect our human need to make sense out of scattered experiences, and to thereby instill meaning, form, order, and assurance.

One of Reagan's chief speechwriters, Peggy Noonan, aptly notes that presidential speeches are part theater and part political or policy declarations. Notable public speeches from Patrick Henry and Lincoln to William Jennings Bryan, FDR, Kennedy, and Martin Luther King Jr. play a role in how we tell each other who we are. "Another reason speeches are important," Noonan speculates, is "because the biggest problem in America is loneliness. A great speech from a leader to the people eases our isolation, breaks down the walls, includes people. It takes them inside a spinning thing and makes them part of the gravity."[6]

President Bill Clinton occasionally displayed patriotic and unifying symbolism, such as when he spoke in Oklahoma City in the aftermath of the tragic bombing of the Alfred P. Murrah Federal Building on April 19, 1995. He also stirred people and summoned pride when he spoke at Southern black Baptist churches and reminded people of the Lincoln and Martin Luther King Jr. legacies.

One of the failings of the George W. Bush presidency was his inability to capture the nation's imagination through his talks and speeches. He attempted to do so in his second inaugural address in 2005, and his theme then about the centrality of liberty and freedom was well received. But he typically looked uncomfortable if not insincere when he occasionally tried to rally the nation in the cause of his initiatives.

Senator Barack Obama's appeal in the 2008 presidential campaign was based in part on his skillful evocation of the restless American yearning for movement and progress. Like JFK and Reagan before him, he talked—often movingly—about the promise of needed change, the promise of a new way of conducting politics, and the promise of including everyone in the blessings of the American Dream.

Obama was criticized for his sometimes dreamy rhetoric or for spinning "just words" as opposed to offering specific solutions—yet his message of hope and change and a heartfelt belief in a better America resonated with many—especially younger—Americans, who were hungering for new leadership and vision.

The Symbolic Presidency

Much of this commingling of the political and of the culturally symbolic in presidential performance is an altogether understandable human response to societal yearnings. Leaders sometimes have no choice but to fulfill tribal roles, no matter how pragmatic, educated, sophisticated, or secular the society. Rituals are ceaselessly reinvented by the human heart.

It may be, in fact, that Americans need more symbolic or ritualistic leadership than many societies simply because we prohibited royalty and the establishment of a state religion. Even many of our Western democratic allies find it desirable to separate their head-of-state functions from their legislative and political leadership functions. Thus England has her queen and her prime minister. Germany has a president to perform head-of-state roles and a chancellor as politician-in-chief.

We do it our own way—and we may pay a price for this union of sometimes conflicting roles in the same office. Indeed, the rise and enlargement of the symbolic features of the American presidency raise a number of problems.

First, presidents are tempted to engage a bit too much in symbolic leadership at the expense of political leadership. Understandably, presidents enjoy the symbolic and ceremonial duties. In the performance of these functions they represent the whole people. As political and partisan leaders they often have to divide us. Much of the job of a president requires setting priorities, building new coalitions around these priorities, hiring and firing top personnel, bargaining with Congress, persuading interest group leaders, and, in general, negotiating compromises with other prominent leaders at home and abroad. These tasks require a president to take controversial stands and make tough political decisions. They also require a president to work closely with party leaders and implement party platform ideas. In short, they require a president, not just to preside, but to take risks, not just to attend ceremonies and give sermons, but to engage in conflict. As head of state and symbol-in-chief, a president seeks to unite us, reassure us, and emphasize order, stability, and continuity. As a political executive, a president has to confront problems, antagonize opponents, and stir us from our complacency.

The relationship between these presidential responsibilities is uneasy. Most of the time a president manages to combine the offices of chief of state and political and party leader without too much difficulty. Most Americans probably understand that a president holds these diverse roles, moving from one to the other as conditions demand. There is nothing wrong with the symbolic powers that come with the job. They can become a problem, however, when they lead the public to believe symbolism equals accomplishment, or when ceremonial and symbolic requirements keep presidents from performing their other demanding duties.

Second, sometimes a president invokes the warrior, priest, and defender-of-the-faith images that come with the job in order to lend legitimacy to decisions or actions that are not deserving of our approval. Perhaps Richard Nixon's enemies list, his deceptiveness in obstructing the judicial investigation of the Watergate break-in, and his extensive invocation of executive privilege best illustrate abuse of the office. Nixon portrayed himself as a leader, like Lincoln, embattled in crisis and needing more deference, loyalty, secrecy, and imperial authority. For a while he was able to get away with this. Fortunately, some of the accountability mechanisms in our system rose to the challenge—but not without difficulty and delay.

Third, the amplification of the symbolic roles of the American presidency may do a disservice in diminishing competing forms of democratic leadership. Our system was not designed to achieve the acquiescence of the many to the rule of a favored few. It is sometimes said that people are ruled by their imaginations; yet it is perhaps more valid to suggest they are governed by the weaknesses of their imaginations. Especially in the age of television and the Internet, our presidents loom so large as to dominate much of the public discourse. It is difficult for political rivals to get air time to present alternative interpretations of what might be desirable policy. The dominant symbolic and priestly roles of presidents sometimes make even the most constructive opposition seem like acts of disloyalty, disobedience, or even sacrilege.

No one, certainly not the founding politicians, ever intended for presidents to be the sole interpreter of the meaning of America. We want a nation that is capable of rich dialogue about our purposes and future aspirations. We also want a nation of leaders, not a nation dependent on a single leader and a single, centralized leadership institution. Our strength has always come from our diversity, our willingness and eagerness to debate and to accept dissenting views as legitimate. A top-heavy leadership structure with undue reverence and deference to the presidency would undermine much that is precious to the American experiment.[7]

If the profound symbolism of the presidency has costly implications for the quality of the relationship between citizens and the presidency, it affects fully as much the ways in which presidents and their associates conceive of themselves and their jobs. The reverence and loyalty rendered a new president are a rich resource, but an overindulgent citizenry can distort the president's psychological perspective and sense of right and wrong. At the height of Watergate, Arthur M. Schlesinger Jr. suggested that what the country needed, in fact, was a considered disrespect for the office of the president, "a refusal to give any weight to a president's words than to the intelligence of the utterance, if spoken by anyone else, would command."[8]

Fortunately, Americans have an excellent appreciation for humor—and our chief deflators of presidential pomposity or phony religiosity are sometimes our cartoonists, comedians, and satirical columnists. A president who goes too far must beware of Garry Trudeau, Jay Leno, Jon Stewart, and Maureen Dowd—to name just a few potential adversaries. Thank God for our robust First Amendment.

On balance, we turn to presidents for more symbolic meaning and ritual leadership than was ever intended—and more than is probably desirable. Such dependency has consequences. Some of these have been reviewed. Doubtless there are additional side effects and implications. We will strengthen the presidency and our constitutional democracy if we have a greater appreciation of the unintended as well as those intended consequences of this profoundly important leadership office.[9]

Chapter Three
Overcoming Groupthink, the Separation of Brain and State, and Machiavelli's Flattery Conundrum

> Philosopher-kings there never have been and never will be, except in the Platonic imagination. And yet every man who thinks seriously . . . about the problems of society finds himself groping toward some reconciling of action and reflection. . . . [T]hough this will never happen, we can come as close to it as reality allows by maintaining good communications and open highways between the citadels of power and the citadels of reflection.
>
> —Former U.S. cabinet member John W. Gardner[1]

One of the primary functions of the president of the United States is to serve as a teacher, as someone who will point the way to unrealized possibilities and to enlighten the nation about realistic priorities. To serve as a teacher or educator, the president has to be an uncommon learner. Much of the institutional presidency in modern times is organized around the tasks of gathering, sorting, and making sense out of large bodies of information.

Our other political institutions have well-defined ways of learning on a regular basis. Thus the Supreme Court learns from formal oral argument, from materials submitted to it from contending sides of a case as well as from lower courts, from judicial conference meetings that involve peer discussions, and from advice gained from law clerks and from new legal research.[2]

Members of Congress learn from a variety of sources. Chief among these are learning from their colleagues (especially like-minded party and home state colleagues), from their staffs, from testimony and research presented at hearings, and from trips and countless communications from constituents back in their districts. Members of Congress also learn from the communications sent to them from the White House and cabinet officials.

Over the past two generations, a somewhat predictable learning process has evolved for presidents. The following are some of the major learning and advising routines that shape how presidents learn:

1. Senior staff memoranda and briefing sessions (especially intelligence and economic estimates)
2. Cabinet advocacy and counsel
3. Congressional party leadership meetings
4. Advocacy from leading business and economic leaders
5. Discussions with (and communications from) other heads of state
6. Reports and counsel from presidential advisory and independent study commissions

7. Proposals and ideas from the Washington bureaucracy
8. Advocacy from interest groups, political action committees, and political movements
9. Lessons learned from the mistakes and successes of former presidents
10. New books and inventions that come to the attention of the White House
11. Suggestions and especially criticism from intellectuals and opposition political leaders
12. Public opinion survey data
13. Newspaper, media, and Internet opinion and interpretation
14. Contact and conversations with friends and citizens at large

Presidents learn also from what is going on within the Congress, within the parties, and from messages sent by the various courts.

Note, however, that there are few systematized procedures. Each president devises anew the learning process, and each decides how much time and how much White House energy are devoted to learning. Still, the process has become reasonably institutionalized. That is, processes have become established in one administration and more or less passed on and adopted or adapted by succeeding administrations.[3] Often there are congressionally mandated reports or requirements that help to enforce institutionalization. Political and media expectations sometimes also encourage the continuation of some of these practices. In this chapter I comment on and raise questions about certain aspects of the presidential learning process. I suggest the following:

1. Much of what the president learns is learned after winning election to the White House.
2. Most of what is important to learn often comes from outside the normal inner circle of the presidential advisory system.
3. A strain exists between intellectuals and creative entrepreneurs and the political leadership in the nation. What may be called a separation of brain and state often exists, and while it is inevitably in tension, presidents and their close advisers need to work to make sure that the separation is not maiming.
4. The use of presidential advisory commissions makes considerable sense and should be used carefully yet frequently.

Unpreparedness of New Presidents

Most U.S. presidents in recent years have come from governorships or from the U.S. Senate. In such positions, these future presidents have obviously learned about many of the more important problems facing the nation. Yet seldom have they developed extensive expertise about major policy issues—especially issues of international economics, trade policy specifics, arms control, and complex developments in distant regions of the world.

To campaign for the White House requires mostly a general knowledge of the controversies of the day. The same questions are endlessly asked by the media, and candidates seldom deviate much from their stump speeches. Many of the issues discussed and debated in the campaign cease to be critical issues after the election. Indeed, many of the major problems and crises that arise during a presidential term are new or unexpected issues.

John F. Kennedy, for example, did not discuss what he would do in Vietnam during his 1960 campaign. He mentioned Vietnam just once or twice in passing. The pressing issue in 1960 was what to do in Quemoy and Matsu, islands off of Formosa. That issue was widely debated, but it was not controversial once Kennedy came to the White House. Vietnam, on the other hand, became one of Kennedy's greatest tests.

Lyndon Johnson had even less preparation for foreign policy responsibilities, and this deficiency later became evident. Countless other new and demanding issues arose during his presidency, even after he was elected to his first full term. One such matter was crime policy. Neither Johnson nor anyone else on his White House staff knew much about the country's crime problem, the criminal justice system, or crime research. The crime issue was raised or generated by Barry Goldwater and others; Johnson and his advisers first tried to ignore it. But that strategy failed, and they groped with considerable unease toward some form of political response to the crime issue. While responding to the issue, they often ignored most of the problem. Eventually the Johnson administration made a number of token or symbolic gestures to assuage public anxiety and to deflate Barry Goldwater's use of the issue.

Richard Nixon won the presidency in 1968 by claiming he had some kind of secret plan to end the Vietnam War. It took four years and numerous new plans, as Nixon was to discover. Jimmy Carter claimed in 1976 that he had ideas about reforming the federal bureaucracy and simplifying the budget process. He, like Ronald Reagan, said that he would balance the budget. George W. Bush was understandably unprepared for the September 11, 2001, attacks on America. Somehow the job's complexities are always more than a match for a candidate's campaign pledges. A president's learning curve is indeed steep.

The impression is often conveyed (an impression fostered by presidential public relations aides) that presidents and their staffs are more informed and better advised than they really are. Again and again, however, presidents and their staffs have to embark upon major exercises in self-education after the election. The reasons are simple. First, to win an election requires general responses to general issues. But policymaking and decision making require much greater understanding of root problems and alternative policy responses and their consequences. Second, many of the major issues facing presidents are issues that were only superficially treated, if raised at all, in the election (for example, Vietnam, Iraq, Central America, and terrorism).[4]

Another reason presidents and their staffs must learn so much is that the pace of change has dramatically increased. Policy proposals that have been posed in a campaign or in the first year of a presidency often become obsolete, overtaken both by events and technological changes. The problems mutate or metastasize and often require a different approach. Such challenges as Social Security, arms control, global warming, and homeland security change with changing circumstances.

Moreover, the aides and supporters a candidate needs to win the White House are often decidedly different from the advisers a president needs to govern and lead. Delegate hunters, political brokers, and campaign strategists are gradually replaced, at least in part, by policy advisers and experts—and the latter often take a while before they can understand a president's style and contribute productively to the president's new learning processes. It took a year or more before Carter became adjusted to his policy staffs in 1977–1978. George W. Bush went through three attorneys general and three treasury secretaries and had regular White House turnover—at least four press secretaries, for example.

Presidents are generalists. The best we probably can expect is that they are bright and curious, ask good questions, and can make sensible and quick decisions when they are pressed to do so. We can hope, too, that they have an evidence-based rather than faith-based way of reasoning. It is justifiably expected in addition that they have the ability to recruit gifted advisers and that they are reasonably quick studies. We should certainly look for presidents who will avoid "groupthink" tendencies, who can develop some form of competing advisory systems (sometimes called multiple advocacy processes), and avoid dogmatic and simpleminded approaches to the crucial task of learning about or rethinking national policy choices.

The dangers of groupthink were famously discussed in Irving Janis's instructive 1972 book *Victims of Groupthink*. It refers to the very human psychological drive for consensus at any cost that can suppress dissent and the rigorous appraisal of policy alternatives in cohesive decision-making groups.[5] Janis contends that poor decisions resulting in some of our nation's worst policy disasters such as the Bay of Pigs and Vietnam escalation have occurred because of defective decision-making processes.

Every president has some advisers who are bearers of consistently good news and what they believe the president wants to hear. Also, "[e]ven the most distinguished and forthright adviser is usually reluctant to stand alone," writes JFK aide Ted Sorensen. If that adviser "fears his persistence in a meeting will earn him the disapprobation of his colleagues, a rebuff by the President, or (in the case of a 'leak') the outrage of the Congress, press, or public, he may quickly seek the safety of greater numbers."[6]

Initial evidence suggests that George W. Bush's decision to wage war in Iraq may have been the product of similar defects in presidential learning and deliberative processes.[7]

If knowledge is power, and it is, the constant challenge for those in the White House is to reach out to those who can supply more explanations and understanding. Information is invariably incomplete. Uncertainty is ever present—so much so that knowing what you do not know is often the first step in the right direction. Asking the right questions becomes critical. A problem well stated, as an old adage has it, is a problem half solved. Knowing when and where to turn for advice is similarly crucial. FDR famously relied upon a "kitchen cabinet" of brain-trusters, friends, and colleagues of his wife as informal advisers and allies to supplement his formal channels of advice.

What we may conclude with certainty is that, despite the growth of White House staff, the executive office of the president, and staff organizations like the Office of Management and Budget, Council of Economic Advisors, and Council on Environmental Quality, every four years the institutionalized White House needs to be reorganized, restaffed, and revitalized as an institution for learning.

Broadly Dispersed Leadership

Policy leadership seldom originates at the White House. Ideas come from a variety of sources—from experiments in states or in other nations, from research breakthroughs, from think tanks, from enterprising members of Congress and their staffs who have been on the outlook for new ideas, from interest groups, and from political movements in the country.

Generally speaking, presidents and their top aides are brokers. They have fought to win election by appealing in broad terms to as many groups and sections of the nation as possible. They have viewed their campaign as a fight to win plurality and majority support—and not as an occasion for adult education or for stirring up divisiveness in the nation. Most of the time, too, they have skillfully phrased much of what they might do in ambiguous terms: "I shall go to Korea"; "Let's get the nation moving again"; "I have a secret plan to end the war"; "I am not a lawyer, I am not from Washington, and I will not lie to you"; and "We need to change the way we do things in Washington."

Breakthrough ideas seldom are invented at the White House. It is much like the invention of new ideas in the private sector. The large so-called expert organizations often get bypassed by smaller, newer, more risk-taking and entrepreneurial outfits. Thus the automobile was not invented by the transportation experts of that era, the railroads. The airplane was not invented by the automobile experts. Polaroid self-developing film was not invented by Kodak. Hand-held pocket calculators were not invented by IBM. Digital watches were not invented by the watchmakers. Apple Computers beat IBM for a couple of years in the home computer market. The list is long and the moral is clear.

Domestic policy change often takes place over a lengthy period, and sometimes it seems as though the White House is the last to learn about the pending change. This is in part because we have created a presidency that is necessarily a brokerage institution: It waits for other groups, individuals, and institutions to take the lead. The White House responds to ideas and suggestions for change, yet usually not until such ideas or proposals have gathered substantial public support. It took almost eight years for George W. Bush, for example, to develop even minimalistic initiatives on carbon emissions and climate change problems.

In many ways, presidents are followers as much as they are leaders. Presidents plainly have to exercise decisive leadership in emergency situations and often in secretive national security activities. Presidents often can assist those who are advocating change. They can nurture or facilitate a national debate and in doing so can often help expand the public support for an idea whose time has yet to come.

Still, most presidents, in common with most elected officials, most of the time are cautious. They fear being in advance of their times. They are tremendously concerned with appearing prudent, practical, sensible, and effective. Thus they act upon ideas for which they can gain congressional passage, or public opinion support, or compliance. Presidents are keen not to fritter away their political capital on futile measures.

Presidents Cleveland and McKinley, for example, were not leaders of the women's suffrage movement. Presidents from Hoover to Kennedy can hardly be called civil rights leaders. Nixon was hardly an environmentally concerned person, and he most assuredly was not an antiwar leader. Nor were presidents in the 1970s advocates of tax cutting. Yet during all of these periods, policy leadership and policy incubation was going on in the nation—often in highly activist and vigorous ways.

Policy ideas often go through a series of stages or acts prior to their gaining acceptance by a president or a presidential candidate. I find helpful the idea of borrowing from the theater to suggest that policy change requires leadership in at least two, three, or even more distinct phases. This oversimplifies and suggests an all-too-tidy frame of reference, yet it is a step in the right direction. Just as there are typically a few acts in most plays, I will illustrate policy leadership as moving along in three acts, and being nurtured or carried by fairly distinctive kinds of leaders.

Act I	*Act II*	*Act III*
Agitators	Coalition builders	Officeholders
Inventors	Consciousness raisers	Elected politicians
Crowd gatherers	Lobbyists	Policymakers
Policy prophets	Movement organizers	White House staff
Movement founders	Policy advocates	Party leaders

Act I leaders are classic crowd gatherers and agitators. They stir things up, raise new and often troublesome ideas, and are often viewed as cranks, rebels, and revolutionaries. Patrick Henry, Samuel Adams, and Thomas Paine provided some of this Act I leadership as a prelude to the American Revolution. Nat Turner and John Brown provided dramatic nineteenth-century civil rights agitation. Howard Jarvis in the 1970s agitated for property tax relief in California. Saul Alinsky, Rachel Carson, Jonathan Schell, and Michael Harrington also illustrate the Act I types. Eco-terrorists such as the Earth Liberation Front inspired by author Edward Abbey are yet other examples of what I mean by Act I "leaders." Peace activist Cindy Sheehan and her efforts to end the war in Iraq is yet another example. Dr. Jack Kevorkian, the activist physician who was jailed for nearly a decade for advocating and overseeing assisted suicides, was also an Act I leader.

Few Act I types get elected to public office or even care about getting elected. Many of them are kept at a distance by the politicians of their eras. Yet all of them catalyzed protests or generated ideas in ways that aroused large numbers of would-be citizen activists.

Act II leaders are the coalition builders. Their ranks include Susan Anthony, Martin Luther King Jr., Jack Kemp, Jerry Falwell, Ralph Nader, and anti–Vietnam War leader Allard Lowenstein. The leaders of the temperance, progressive, populist, consumer rights, anti–Vietnam War, nuclear freeze, Moral Majority and antiglobalization movements and activists like the protestors in Seattle in 1999 are all Act II actors. Usually unelected and unelectable, they galvanize movements and coalitions in such a compelling way that politicians at least begin to heed their message and listen—even if only coolly at first. In the 2008 presidential nominating campaigns, libertarian Republican congressman Ron Paul (TX) and leftish Democratic congressman Dennis Kucinich (Ohio) were distinctive Act II type voices outlining valid yet contrarian policy initiatives. Act II actors educate, raise interest, and enlarge the ranks of their supporters. They wish to publicize new ideas (and sometimes to revive old ideas) and bring pressure on those who serve in the White House and other political establishment centers.

Act III leaders typically are elected officials. Some have highly publicized and sometimes even glamorous careers. But the Act III types heed public opinion as much as mold it. Act III types are typically more constrained than the nonelected political leaders, and they often find themselves dependent on Act I and Act II leaders for fresh thinking and novel approaches to public problems. Act III leaders invariably become enmeshed in the challenge of reconciling competing claims about the public interest. They must think and act within the bounds of what is pragmatic and what can be accomplished. Bill Clinton and both George W. Bush and his father were all classic Act III types with the possible exception of George W. Bush's preventive war in Iraq. Each of them won narrow elections, worried a lot about public opinion, and time and again backed down when their domestic policy "reforms" (such as health care, Social Security, or immigration policies) came under opposition. Each also was hesitant to become a leader on genocide and global warming matters.

The most serious charge against many of the Act III types is that they are simply fixers, bargainers, transactional brokers, and Johnny-come-latelys. They are often pictured as lacking strong convictions and moving in whatever direction the wind is blowing, as opportunists willing to sell out to the highest bidder in money or votes. The charge is usually overdrawn, but a core of truth remains: Act III types and the occupants of the White House not only are brokers but have to be bargainers and agreement makers in order to make the system work. The American political system has so much built-in conflict, so many representatives of competing or warring constituencies, and so many checks and balances that compromise at the highest levels is inevitable. More often than not, this frustrates the expectations of Act I and II leaders.

Presidents are frequently criticized for not providing leadership for all scenes, for all acts, for all seasons. A more refined appreciation of how our political system is fashioned would lead to a recognition that most presidents most of the time have to operate in the Act II-and-a-half to Act III range. They are necessarily dependent on other types of leaders to generate the inventions and the movements that help the nation to renew and change itself. We would all be better judges of presidents if we recognized the considerable degree to which leadership in this nation is dispersed and that much of the leadership we need—at least on many occasions—is not leadership from the top, but in local and state governments, or indeed outside of government altogether, in movement, group, and entrepreneurial grassroots leadership from outside of Washington and outside of government.

Note that sometimes an individual may move from one act to another. Thus a Reverend Jesse Jackson, for example, performs Act I functions when he is an outspoken advocate, Act II functions when he is an organizer of Operation Push, and in 1984 he very nearly became an Act III operative as he sought the Democratic Party's nomination for the presidency. Ralph Nader operated in Act I or Act I-and-a-half when he wrote *Unsafe at Any Speed,* the book that condemned General Motors and its shoddy automobiles and its neglect of automobile safety. Nader was an Act II type when he organized research and advocacy activities and recruited money and staff to lobby for his political agenda. And Nader was a would-be, if somewhat implausible, Act III type as he sought the presidency in 2000 and other election years. Both Hillary Clinton and Barack Obama were Act II policy activists working on behalf of children's and women's rights and poor neighborhoods before they became elected legislators and then presidential candidates.

Former U.S. senator and vice president Al Gore is a curious example of someone who was predominantly an Act III leader, yet was persistently an Act II educator and catalyst on crucial environmental issues both before and after serving as a generally conventional vice president. His notable documentary and book *An Inconvenient Truth* (2006) were distinctively Act II in message and character.

Important leadership comes from all three acts. Presidents may be dependent, more than either they or we realize, on

Act I and II types for ideas and new initiatives—but so also the Act I and II types must depend on presidents or other national Act III leaders to bring about the compromise or brokered decisions that permit needed change or breakthroughs in legislation, court decisions, or executive actions. Act III leadership can be just as creative and innovative as leadership in Act I or II. Similarly officials in Act III can fail because of caution or ineptitude, just as Act I and II types can fail in their undertakings. The lesson is that leadership rarely comes from a single person or a single institution. Leadership is dispersed, and leaders are extraordinarily dependent on other leaders to help shape, develop, enact, and implement the policy changes the nation needs.

Separation of Brain and State

There are countless definitions of an intellectual. These range from the uncharitable description of intellectuals as people who take more words than necessary to say more than they know, to the more general definition of the intellectual as a person devoted to matters of the mind, to study, reflection, and speculation. Arthur M. Schlesinger Jr. suggests an "intellectual is a person happy with ideas, likes them, thinks about them, talks about them, and worries about them."[8] Intellectuals like to build ideas up, break them down, refine them, and, in the larger sense, connect ideas together to build theories about the meaning of life, the universe, truth, beauty, and justice.

An intellectual is also in part a philosopher, a lover of truth and knowledge; someone interested in ideas for the love of wisdom; someone who has an innate love and curiosity for knowledge and seeks ends beyond the immediate practical needs of society. Intellectuals question the truth of the moment and view things in the longer, higher, and wider sense of "truth" and "justice." In short, intellectuals, in the tradition of Socrates and Plato, dream of what might be, of what ought to be. This nation was shaped and founded in large part by a number of intellectual activists. John Adams, Benjamin Franklin, Alexander Hamilton, Thomas Jefferson, James Wilson, James Madison, and scores of others helped organize the ideas that empowered this new Republic. But, more often than not, the intellectual has played a detached role, often skeptical, critical, or even outraged by the misuses and abuses of power. This is not always the case. Many, like Aristotle, have been tutors to great statesmen. In our time, we have had Roosevelt's brains trust and scores of John Kenneth Galbraiths and Edward Tellers, as well as individuals like Arthur Burns, Arthur Okun, Henry Kissinger, Daniel Patrick Moynihan, and advisers like Arthur M. Schlesinger Jr., Zbigniew Brzezinski, Martin Feldstein, Jeane Kirkpatrick, and Condoleezza Rice.[9]

What Theodore White once hailed in 1967 as the rise of the "action-intellectuals" also poses some problems. Can an intellectual become involved in the exercise of power without losing the perspective and perhaps even the credentials of a disinterested scholar? Walter Lippmann suggested this was risky business: "It is only knowledge freely acquired that is disinterested. When, therefore, men whose profession it is to teach and investigate become the makers of policy, become members of an administration in power, become politicians and leaders of causes, they are committed. Nothing they can say can be relied upon as disinterested. Nothing they can teach can be trusted as scientific." Lippmann added, "It is impossible to mix the pursuit of knowledge, and those who have tried it turn out to be very bad politicians or they cease to be scholars."[10]

Some observers go even beyond Lippmann's point and say that the essence of intellectual thinking is disagreement. Solzhenitsyn writes, "The task of the artist is to sense more keenly than others the harmony of the world, the beauty and the outrage of what man has done to it, and poignantly to let people know."[11]

Intellectuals as critics commonly disparage the things associated with politics. Manipulation, compromise, pragmatism, wheeling and dealing, coercion, and the endless bickering and squabbling that make up the practice of politics leave the intellectual indifferent or hostile. Henry David Thoreau wrote that what is called politics "is comparatively so superficial and inhuman that practically I have never fairly recognized it concerns me at all."[12] Intellectuals often dismiss politicians as persons who either became chronic liars or are too prone to limit rather than expand horizons. "All of the major politicians are interchangeable. They are all paid for more or less by the same people, and they do not even pretend now to be representative of the people at large."[13]

Woodrow Wilson saw it this way: "The men who act stand nearer to the mass of men than do the men who write. ... The men who write love proportion, the men who act must strike out practical lines of action and neglect proportion; here, unquestionably, we come upon the heart of the perennial misunderstanding." Wilson in the 1912 campaign went on to say, "What I fear is a government of experts. God forbid that in a democratic country we should resign the task and give the government over to the experts."[14]

We are unlikely to realize Wilson's fear. Still, there are serious questions. Presidents must recognize tension between the men of action and the men of thought and what Wilson called the perennial and persisting misunderstandings. Yet presidents and their closest lieutenants should also make efforts to encourage the creative inventors in the land. This nation has remained great in part because it has been, on the whole, an open society—a society where ideas are encouraged and where the dissenter in politics as well as in the arts and sciences is free to innovate and develop fresh ideas and fresh approaches. The challenge is how to encourage intellectuals, inventors, and researchers (and artists and poets) to contribute positive and constructive as well as critical ideas, to suggest and point a way toward ideas that might make our constitutional democracy stronger and more responsive.

Intellectuals doubtless will be gadflies, outsiders, and critics commonly immune to the seductions of power. Some have even suggested that their powerlessness is the precondition to their being imaginative. The transcending intellectual is a questioner always concerned with the higher goals, purposes, and values of both society and humankind. At their best, they are often a shadow or opposition government—in the best sense of those phrases. Poet Percy Bysshe Shelley, even if it was self-indulgent, went so far as saying "poets are the unacknowledged legislators of the world."[15] Solzhenitsyn adds, "The great writer is, so to speak, a second government; that's why no regime anywhere has ever loved its great writers, only its minor ones."[16] One way writers, in Act I or early Act II, make a major contribution to political discourse is through provocative pamphlets or books that either call attention to public policy problems or call on people to rally around the possibilities of a better America. The power of the pen in the hands of Thomas Paine, Harriet Beecher Stowe, Upton Sinclair, Michael Harrington, Rachel Carson, Milton Friedman, and Edward Abbey, to cite just a few examples, surely made up for their lack of the power of the purse or the sword.

Presidential Advisory Commissions

The conventional solution for information-starved presidents is to build up their White House staffs. This has been done extensively since the time of FDR. But there are limits to the number of useful staff a president can have. After a while the addition of more and more staff units and cabinet councils often merely multiplies a president's managerial problems without giving valuable service in return. Giving a president more staff often actually insulates a president from currents of thought he or she should be aware of—both within the government and from outside. Sadly much of the recent growth in the presidential staff has been public relations or promotional staffs primarily engaged in marketing and "spinning" presidential positions.[17]

It is fashionable in journalistic circles to poke fun at presidential commissions. But they are also one of the solutions to the need for enhanced presidential learning. Not all presidential commissions have worked out well, yet, more often than not, these short-term advisory groups have added to presidential and national learning. They are one way to overcome the potential separation of brain and state. If they have not worked as well as they should have, why this has been so needs to be examined. The effectiveness of outside advisory units rests upon a variety of factors, especially these:

- Policymakers who genuinely want good policy intelligence
- The determination and definition of a worthy need for outside advisers
- Recruitment of appropriately talented and concerned members

- Intelligent staffing and relevant briefings
- Informed analysis and high-level independent analysis of the resulting reports and recommendations; an opportunity for public debate and criticism

Presidential advisory commissions were essentially a twentieth-century creation.[18] There have been hundreds of White House–level advisory commissions since the 1930s. They are ad hoc rather than permanent in nature. Research indicates that commissions are generally created by presidents who seriously want policy advice and want to learn. We find that most presidents, with some notable exceptions, act favorably on the reports they receive from commissions. The conventional wisdom is often the opposite: namely, those presidents appoint commissions and similar study groups in order to avoid issues, delay action, or to deflect public attention. Members of Congress are sometimes jealous of this practice because they view it as a legislative responsibility to gather ideas by holding hearings, conducting investigations, and using other methods devised by Congress to fulfill its constitutional mandate.

Presidents have created national commissions to study Social Security reform, foreign aid, civil rights, NASA disasters such as the 1986 *Challenger* launch, HIV/AIDS, and a Bill Clinton–appointed National Commission to Ensure a Strong and Competitive Airline Industry.[19]

Congress more recently has forced presidents, such as George W. Bush, to establish commissions to investigate controversies such as the September 11, 2001, terrorist attacks and the decisions to wage preventive war against Iraq in 2003.

President George W. Bush tried to block some of these congressional efforts, fearing that questions of policymaking errors might reveal things that should be kept secret or at least would divert the public's attention from homeland security priorities.

The Bush administration worked hard to limit the effectiveness of the 9/11 Commission led by Lee Hamilton and Tom Kean in 2004.[20] Similarly, the Bush administration largely ignored the key Baker-Hamilton recommendations in the 2006 *Iraq Study Group Report*.

The *Iraq Study Group Report* was the brainchild of members of Congress who reached out to nonprofit groups such as the Center for the Study of the Presidency and the Center for Strategic and International Studies. Republican senator John Warner gave it his blessing, as did, in a lukewarm way, President Bush.

For more than eight months in 2006, the Iraq Study Group reviewed the controversial Iraq war and occupation and proposed pragmatic strategies for achieving peace and stability in Iraq. It brought together an impressive, bipartisan group of elder statespeople to clarify America's national interests in Iraq. As former national security adviser General Brent Scowcroft put it, this report "outlined with clarity and precision the key factors at issue in Iraq."[21]

George Bush's response to this congressionally initiated commission was to be quietly polite in receiving their advice, but privately he signaled he thought their advice impractical. One of Bush's closest top aides and friends suggested the president would continue to do what he thought was right and that his decisions very often would be contrary to the Iraq Study Group's recommendations. Said Andrew Card, "The president by definition knows more than any of those people who are serving on those panels."[22]

Occasionally, presidents have used commissions for other purposes. In practice, a variety of motives or concerns prompt presidents to create these commissions. A commission is created:

1. When a president needs outside help to analyze a controversial question because his own top officials are not providing enough information.
2. When a president genuinely desires a fresh outside perspective and fully intends to offer leadership on the topic when the commission is finished with its work.
3. When the president may not need further information for himself but wants a bipartisan group of experts to help him build bipartisan support for a policy or program initiative.
4. When a controversial issue has to be resolved and a president is less in need of new information than in need of new negotiations and presidential-congressional bargaining.
5. When a president is responding to a major crisis or tragedy (the death of John F. Kennedy, Three Mile Island, the 1986 *Challenger* disaster) and needs an investigation that will find answers and reassure the president and the public.
6. When a president (as did Hoover, Eisenhower, and Carter) wishes to forecast trends and anticipate new challenges and possible solutions.

Defining the success or effectiveness of national or presidential commissions is not easy, for one has to take into account the variety of purposes for which they are used. Some are useful for their findings. Some are useful for the general education they provide, like Milton Eisenhower's Commission on Violence. Some, like the 1982–1983 Social

Security Commission, are useful for legislative initiatives. Others, like the 1983 Kissinger panel on Central America, help survey a thorny situation and may perhaps provide new information and a fresh perspective for both the president and Congress. An outright failure is rare for a presidential commission—as long as the definition of success is broadly defined. We should rightly ask how these commissions may affect the existing channels for helping presidents to learn. Does reliance on advisory commissions diminish the vitality of the cabinet, the various units in the executive office of the president, or even the Congress? This is probably not the case, but this question needs study. Sometimes members of Congress have served on these commissions. Moreover, Congress can always appoint its own commissions, and, as noted, it has occasionally done this. A performance shoot-out (to borrow an IBM term) between presidential and congressionally appointed commissions might occasionally be a productive competition.

Commissions, when properly designed, can be a useful device for bridging some of the gap between those who are detached thinkers and researchers and those who have to make practical decisions in the world of government. They can also sometimes serve as a catalyst to raise questions or to pose issues for further research. James Sundquist of the Brookings Institution rightly called for more attention to be paid to what he called research brokerage—the people or institutions who can translate research findings and information into the kinds of usable information that policymakers can readily absorb.[23] A proliferation of think tanks in recent decades, building on the earlier models of the Brookings Institution and the Hoover Institution, is helping somewhat to perform this function. Federal government laboratories and similar research organizations such as the RAND Corporation are also part of the solution here. Doubtless, however, more intermediaries of this kind will be needed going forward.

Presidential commissions—such as those on the MX missile or the Commission for the Study of Ethical Problems in Medicine and Biomedical and Behavioral Research—obviously pose vital policy problems, problems that cry out for more attention from the nation's researchers, inventors, and citizens at large.

The George W. Bush presidency illustrates a variety of flawed decision-making processes. The decision to invade Iraq, the failure to anticipate Hurricane Katrina, and the clumsy efforts to deal with Social Security, immigration, stem-cell research, and global warming all raised questions about presidential and White House learning.

Writing about the flawed use of and politicization of policy intelligence on Iraq decisions in the Bush White House, political scientist James P. Pfiffner concludes: "Although there is no guarantee that a sound decision-making process or accurately interpreting intelligence will ensure wise policy decisions, we have learned from this experience that the analytical objectivity of the intelligence community must be protected if policy makers are to base their decisions on realistic evaluations of our adversaries' behavior. The lack of a deliberative decision-making process and the compromising of the objectivity of the intelligence community can lead to disaster."[24]

Two additional yardstick lessons might well be memorialized on the walls of the White House's west wing. First, the playwright Sophocles' injunction that a king whose ears are sealed by fear and is unwilling to seek advice is damned.[25] Second, from a convicted former Nixon White House aide, Egil Krogh, who belatedly recognized that sincerity and loyalty to a president "can often be as blinding as worthy."

Krogh's advice to all who will work for a president is: "I hope they will recognize that the banner of national security can turn perceived patriotism into actual disservice. When contemplating a course of action, I hope they will never fail to ask, 'Is this right?'"[26]

In sum, presidents go about learning in a variety of ways. No one way is adequate. Plainly, their styles and temperament affect how, and how much, they learn. But much of their learning takes place after they get to the White House. Much of their learning comes about because of messages sent from a distance rather than coming in neat tidy packages from the West Wing or from across the street in the Executive Office Buildings. An inevitable tension between brain and state often grows worse during presidential terms, and presidents will not easily solve this clash of styles and values. We need to conceive of the potential learning process at the White House in wider, broader terms. Presidents as both learners and educators, and ultimately as teachers, need in a larger sense to encourage the nation to learn along with them and to encourage the nation to help discover the ideas and approaches needed to solve critical national problems.

Chapter Four
President John F. Kennedy: Act III Politician

> It is said that the presidency of the United States is the most powerful office in the world. What is not said or even generally understood is that the power of the chief executive is hard to achieve, balky to manage, and incredibly difficult to exercise.
>
> —John Steinbeck[1]

He dazzled the nation as a politician and as our 34th president. Yet his presidency is difficult to evaluate. His record was mixed. Scholars regularly rank him as an average, or at best, an above-average president. Even he was dissatisfied with his performance, although he was more pleased with his third than with his first two years.

Three things are striking about the way John F. Kennedy is viewed today. First, he is regarded as one of the patron saints of progressives, and yet the revisionists, with some justification, say he did little or nothing to help the truly needy during his three years. At the end of his term most of the poor were still poor, most of the voiceless were still voiceless, and, if anything, the gap between rich and poor had widened. Second, appraisals of his presidency range along a spectrum from reverential books written by his former aides and acquaintances, to the condemnatory rebukes of revisionists on the right and left. Finally, Kennedy's name looms exceedingly large for two generations born after his death, yet few in these can discuss his accomplishments in any detail. Time and again, they will say they believe Kennedy was an effective political leader, a courageous and splendid person, yet—if pressed—they admit they are puzzled or even confused about why he is so memorable.

The analysis that follows treats the myth and the reality with a special focus on Kennedy as a political leader. Kennedy yearned to be more than a conventional politician and orthodox power broker, but to get to the White House he first had to be both. His presidential campaign promised marked change, but perhaps his unusually great popularity in his first two years stems from his deliberately cautious approach to using the powers of his office. It is important to note, in contrast, that in the third year when he began to venture out and let his newer and bolder personal convictions shape more of his leadership, his popularity declined.

Kennedy had written a notable book on the need for courage in politics, and yet he was detached, diffident, and hesitant to let his moral passion affect his decisions. He was intellectually curious and often had an intellectual affinity with the left, yet he disliked the "liberal" label and rarely acted with ideological zeal. Could it be that the calculating broker style he had so artfully employed to win the 1960 election inhibited him from developing the leadership style needed to become the progressive president he yearned to be? This is one of the puzzles of his presidency.

In the end he had an impact on all of us who lived in this country at the time. If nothing else he made people think of politics, the presidency, and government in different ways. His impact in many ways had less to do with conventional legislative or administrative achievements than it did with attitudes, values, and symbols. His ultimate contributions were more than the sum of his policy record in the White House.

His death and the ensuing national grief changed the country's view of him. The real John F. Kennedy vanished on November 22, 1963. What he was and what he achieved and failed to achieve became suppressed by the needs and demands of those who sought something greater for JFK than death: martyrdom. It was hoped that his unfulfilled promises and policies would emerge phoenix-like in the hearts and minds of kindred leaders and in the corridors of power. "In myth he becomes what they want him to have been," writes biographer William Manchester, "and anyone who belittles this transformation has an imperfect understanding of how the emotions of an entire nation may be moved. A romantic concept of what may have been can be far more compelling than what was."[2]

"A nation reveals itself not only by the men it produces," Kennedy himself noted a few weeks before his death, "but also by the men it honors, the men it remembers."[3] We remember him still. Opinion polls regularly show Kennedy as one of the most popular and cherished presidents. Thus, a *New York Times/CBS News* Poll in 1996 asked Americans which president they would like back in the White House. President Kennedy won that poll; Ronald Reagan, Lincoln, and FDR came in way behind him.[4] Franklin D. Roosevelt came in a distant second. More recent polls indicate that the American public's favorite presidents—of all time—are Lincoln, Kennedy, and Ronald Reagan, leaving FDR and Washington, astonishingly, in some lesser category.

No doubt, Kennedy's presidency and the Kennedy legend are accorded a favored and often magical place because of his shocking assassination. The romanticists and court biographers, as well as the revisionists on both the left and the right have had their day—and still Kennedy looms large on the nation's landscape of heroism and leadership. Ultimately, wrote George Orwell, there may be no test of literary merit except survival. So also, perhaps, with public men and how we judge them.

John F. Kennedy would doubtless be taken aback by the inflated view of his presidency and his accomplishments. He would agree with those who say he accomplished less than he set out to. He would decline being placed on the same level with Abraham Lincoln or Franklin D. Roosevelt. He would probably accept the verdict of historians and other analysts that he was an above-average, but not a great or even near-great, president. "If only I could have had a few more years," he might say, "perhaps we could have earned it." He would say his short-lived two years and ten months (1,037 days) had not afforded him enough time or opportunity to display the kind of courage and leadership he wanted.

In effect, Kennedy suggests this notion in his 1963 State of the Union Address when he said, "We cannot be satisfied to rest here. This is the side of the hill not the top. We have made a beginning but we have only begun." He would have been the first to admit his failings, yet he would note failings are easier to see in hindsight. He would have engaged in little self-pity: His father raised him never to indulge this. On the contrary, despite chronic illnesses, Kennedy was remarkably self-possessed. He was always optimistic and nearly always self-confident. Thus he said when he was at the White

House: "Sure it's a big job. But I don't know anybody who can do it better than I can."[5] He would sometimes add: "Plus the pay is good and I can walk to work."

Kennedy would welcome debate about his presidency. He liked spirited discussions about leaders and their use of power, and he often celebrated poets and artists who were skeptical about the use of power. Only the artist and writer can, from a disinterested perspective, determine whether we use power or power uses us, he once said, sounding much like Alexander Solzhenitsyn.

Kennedy appreciated that people outside of government would view things, and should view them, from a different perspective. At Amherst College, he exhibited a subtle understanding for those charged with the pursuit of truth, beauty, and justice. "If art is to nourish the roots of our culture," Kennedy said, "we must set artists free to follow their vision wherever it takes them." "When power leads man toward arrogance, poetry reminds him of his limitations. . . . When power corrupts, poetry cleanses."[6] Thus, in serving their vision of the truth, said Kennedy, writers, composers, and artists ably serve their society.

Kennedy would be puzzled by the wide range of books and interpretations about his short presidency. He would be as annoyed by the hero-worship books as by the books that blame him unfairly for an imperial presidency, for inventing anew or extending the Cold War, or for all else that went wrong in the 1960s and the 1970s. He would express surprise that his presidency affords so many authors so much room for so many varied interpretations. He might postulate that many of the treatments of the Kennedy presidency, or the Kennedy era, tell us as much about the writers who wrote them as they do about him. Their own methodologies or theoretical or ideological preferences often show through loud and clear, and he would be able to cite ample evidence for this proposition.

Realities and Paradoxes

Some basic realities shaped John F. Kennedy. Unquestionably, the most important shaping influence was his father. Joseph P. Kennedy put a remarkably strong stamp on his children. He taught them to have ambition, seek challenge, and love the competitive life. He also raised them to achieve politically and socially what he had achieved financially. He had been snubbed, and he deeply resented being considered a hyphenated Irish-American. He especially resented references to his own father as a bartender and saloon-keeper.

Joe Kennedy dreamed all the dreams associated with the American Dream, including joining the financial and political elite of the nation. Thus, he was deeply hurt when he was not allowed to join a private country club near Boston. He was bruised when Harvard overlooked him for an honorary degree and when he failed to win election to Harvard's Board of Overseers. The discrimination that stemmed from his Irish Catholic background particularly haunted him, and his reaction typically was, "I was born here. My children were born here. What the hell do I have to do to be an American?" Ambassador Kennedy (he was appointed ambassador to Great Britain by FDR) got mad and got even. He sought to assuage his resentment by seeing his sons accepted. They would become politicians in order to become leaders in order to become American statesmen. They had little choice in the matter. Sparing no expense, the senior Kennedy turned his household into a training ground for political leaders. Did the father's social and psychological need for power and acceptance influence his son John? Most assuredly. But for that influence, he could easily have lived a life of pleasure and leisure.

JFK was never a strong student, struggling merely to pass Latin, French, and math. In secondary school he graduated 65th in his 1935 class of 110. In 1930 he had taken an Otis Intelligence Test and scored 119, indicating above-average, yet less than brilliant, intelligence. He attended Princeton for three months in the fall of 1935, dropping out before Christmas presumably because of illness, yet possibly also because of weak performance. A year later he entered Harvard where his record was mostly "gentlemen's Cs" until his last year or two. He failed to come close in a race for president of his Harvard freshman class and thereafter withdrew from campus politics.

Later, as a national politician, Kennedy often seemed more preoccupied with getting there than with the precise issues or goals to be dealt with once arrived. To get to the top in American politics, he knew one had to reflect the nation more than lead it; one had to respond to the dominant moods rather than shake them up and recast them. He became a representative figure in order to make his way to the top. It all came rather easily in some respects, for he was neither a pronounced progressive nor a conservative. If his family had not been so steeped in Democratic Party politics, he could as easily have been a liberal Republican. He liked to view himself as "prudent" (a favorite word of his), as practical, mainstream, and representative. All of these qualities, of course, aided his electability.

Kennedy probably knew that being president demanded what might be termed Act III leadership. If he didn't grasp this notion as a candidate he did so soon after getting there. Act I leaders would stir things up and would champion causes that were well in advance of the times. Act II leaders, such as Martin Luther King Jr., whom Kennedy admired, organized the movements and pushed for changes from the outside. Act III leaders, including most presidents, are destined to be the brokers, the adjusters, the incrementalists who write the laws and make the interpretations in the realm of the achievable. They are accountable to majorities, and they can only occasionally move beyond conventional thinking and popular moods. They can, to be sure, make a difference. They can help set the national agenda, they can raise issues, and they can choose to respond to one particular set of Act II leaders. Many of Kennedy's severest critics mistakenly despair that Kennedy, the mainstream politician, failed to become a leader for all acts. They wanted him to be both an On Broadway and Off Broadway actor-activist at the same time. Still others wanted him to be even more experimental, to be Off-Off Broadway. If he were here today, Kennedy would remind us that the presidency as an institution was designed to provide the balancing brokerage and only occasionally the emergency leadership for the nation. We have to look elsewhere, he would tellingly suggest, for the agitating and conscience-arousing leadership for a nation. If a presidency tries to be all things to all people, and attempts to provide leadership for all the seasons of policy change in America, in the end it will collapse from its own overreaching.

Many of these clashing expectations arise in the study of Kennedy precisely because the presidency itself is a paradoxical institution. We want presidents to be like us, but also better than we are. We yearn for the common man as well as for the uncommon, heroic, charismatic hero. We want presidents to be both programmatic and pragmatic. We want a decent, just, and moral leader, but also a guileful, cunning, and occasionally ruthless leader. The list is long and the moral is vivid—we want all kinds of things from a president, and the job forces presidents to balance competing conceptions of what Americans want: Kennedy brought some of his paradoxes with him—yet they became magnified and added to those coming with the job.

The Politician

Joseph Kennedy knew that a great national leader must first be a successful politician. John Kennedy may have initially been reluctant to run for office, yet in a very real sense, it was in his blood. One of his grandfathers, John F. "Honey Fitz" Fitzgerald, served three terms in Congress (elected in 1894) and was the first Irish American to win election (in 1903) as mayor of Boston. His other grandfather, P. J. Kennedy, served a few terms in the state legislature and was an important political figure in East Boston for several years. John F. Kennedy was involved in campaigns as early as the age of five—doing precinct work in Boston for Grandfather Fitzgerald. His own father had been a key supporter of Franklin Roosevelt in 1931 and 1932, and again in 1936. Joseph P. Kennedy was a major contributor and fund-raiser for FDR. In the mid-1930s he served as the chairman of the Securities and Exchange Commission and later as ambassador to England. He even aspired to the White House himself. Joe Kennedy doubtless viewed himself as more gifted, more intelligent, and more successful than Roosevelt, with whom eventually he had a stormy relationship.

The father believed that, in America, power, opportunity, and political leadership are open to all who have the will to try. He knew too that money helped. The senior Kennedy had made so much money that his sons were never compelled to find success in business. This was the old man's intention. John Kennedy had expected his older brother, Joe

Jr., to enter politics, but Joe died in combat in 1944. John Kennedy, the second son, realized what his father wanted; later he would occasionally quip, "Mothers want their sons to grow up to be president, but they don't want them to become politicians in the process."[7] Well, JFK had a father who insisted he be both a politician and a president.

John F. Kennedy returned from World War II as a minor hero, and within a year friends had drafted him to run for the U.S. Congress. A vacancy created by the early departure of U.S. Representative James Michael Curley (who was running for mayor of Boston) forced a special election in Massachusetts's Eleventh Congressional District. Kennedy ran in a crowded field and came in first. This 1946 victory launched his 17-year career as a professional politician, during which he won five successive races for the House and Senate.

Kennedy was not a natural campaigner at first, and his early speeches were often routine. His boyish good looks and fascinating family, however, made him a curiosity. He also learned to campaign with intensity, and, with ample funds from his father, he began to build a powerful personal political organization. Once elected, however, he was often bored in the House of Representatives, and this boredom, combined with various illnesses, caused frequent absences. He blasted the Truman administration in these years for "losing China," but he had few deep ideological convictions about domestic and foreign policies.

Kennedy was seldom challenged by the routine of the House of Representatives. Even when he was not sick or socializing, he appeared underwhelmed by it most of the time. "We are just worms here," a friend recalls him saying at the time, as if to suggest his insignificance. An even closer friend remembers it this way: "It [the House] totally failed to fascinate him. It really never grabbed him. I think his father may have made one mistake which was to give him an air travel credit card so that he was on the plane to Palm Beach every Friday night during the winter and, of course, up to the Cape in the summer. He seemed to me to stay pretty much on the periphery of House life."[8]

By 1951 he was ready to move on and decided to run either for the Massachusetts governorship or U.S. Senate seat, both of which would be contested in 1952. This required him to build a statewide organization, which Kennedy did with passion. Kennedy, the politician, always took to campaigning with more zeal than to legislating or policymaking. Why did he run? "Not for ideological reasons," writes political scientist and Kennedy biographer James MacGregor Burns. "He was not pursuing an overriding cause or even an arresting new program—that was not his way. His motivating force was mainly his love of campaigning, of beating the odds, of besting the other guy and, above all, of reaching for the highest stakes. It was the ultimate game."[9]

After some hesitation, Kennedy decided to take on Republican senator Henry Cabot Lodge, the epitome of the Yankee Establishment. Old Joe Kennedy urged his son on: "When you've beaten him, you've beaten the best. Why try for something less?"[10] Kennedy aide Larry O'Brien captures John Kennedy as a maturing politician in his memoirs. O'Brien writes that Kennedy canvassed the state for volunteers and campaign workers. He notes that for himself, and many of his friends, this became a historic confrontation between the flower of the Yankee Establishment and "the best that we newer Americans could put forward as our champion." Kennedy and his team deliberately built their own organization, separate from the establishment Democrats. This was done partly because the regulars were not well organized in several areas around the state, and partly because their candidate for governor, Paul Dever, was expected to run less well than Kennedy. John F. Kennedy ran an almost perfect campaign that year, yet it was a year of considerable learning. O'Brien writes: "He could not be called a natural politician; he was too reserved by nature. To stand by a factory gate and shake hands with the workers was never easy for him, nor was he ever fully at ease with the old-style political leaders in Massachusetts. But he knew what he wanted and he would force himself to do whatever was necessary to achieve it. Throughout the 1952 campaign he became more at ease with strangers, a better public speaker and more confident campaigner. . . . Kennedy had talent and he worked hard to perfect it; above all, he was a proud man who took intense pride in every aspect of his work."[11]

An overconfident Lodge spent much of that year campaigning with, and for, Dwight Eisenhower. Only too late did he come home and begin concentrating on his own Senate race. Kennedy won. Kennedy was lucky that year. His father's money and his own political élan seized the advantage that Lodge's absence and complacency yielded. Some people make themselves luckier than others, and luck is rightly defined as when preparation meets opportunity.

Kennedy became a backbencher in the U.S. Senate. He was never a member of what was then called the Senate "inner club." Moreover, he often seemed distracted by his social life, and, again, he was often sick. Still, he was in great demand as a celebrity, for he was a member of the alluring Kennedy clan, and he was its youthful golden boy, a promising young man with a fortune and a future. The longer he stayed in the Senate the more publicity he received, despite his ineffectiveness as a senator.

In Kennedy's only political loss of his career, he allowed his name to be considered at the 1956 Democratic Convention as his party's vice presidential nominee. Kennedy had considered this option for several weeks, yet worried that it might hurt rather than help his later career ambitions. To the surprise of most people, Adlai Stevenson, the party's presidential nominee, threw open to the convention delegates the choice for the "veep" nominee. Kennedy and his advisers waged a valiant and impressive short campaign in Chicago but could only manage a strong second-place finish.

His loss turned out to be a blessing. Had he won, his political career might have been more damaged than helped as he went down to defeat with Stevenson. Moreover, his Catholicism might have been blamed for the magnitude of Stevenson's loss.

Kennedy accepted his defeat gracefully and won enormous national exposure. Speaking briefly and extemporaneously after many sleepless hours, he thanked the hundreds of delegates who had supported him, congratulated Stevenson on his open-convention decision, and proceeded to recommend that Senator Estes Kefauver's nomination as the party's vice president be unanimous. In this brief moment of triumphant defeat, John Kennedy's campaign for the presidency was born. Almost immediately he was in greater demand than ever as a spokesperson and crowd gatherer for the Democratic party. (Years later, Barack Obama's political future was similarly greatly enhanced by his designation as the 2004 keynote speaker at the Democratic National Convention in Boston.)

Once the 1956 election was over, Kennedy, his family, and close friends began plotting a campaign strategy to win the Democratic presidential nomination in 1960. This meant extensive nationwide speaking engagements and private meetings with countless party brokers and machine leaders in all parts of the country. It also meant winning a smashing reelection victory to the Senate in 1958. Kennedy did all this well (he won reelection to the Senate by nearly 74 percent), and in the process he further matured as a political professional. Kennedy even began to like politics and became at least tolerant of all the small talk and brief encounters of a superficial kind. His star was on the rise, and his views, such as they were, began to be taken seriously. Until 1958 Kennedy had primarily been a follower. He was now becoming a leader, and he was challenged by the possibilities. In a 1958 Roper poll, Kennedy, now only 41 years old, won recognition as the most admired man in the U.S. Senate. Other polls began to show him as a top contender for the 1960 Democratic Party presidential nomination.

As he prepared to run for the nomination in 1959, he was widely criticized and heatedly opposed by important factions in the Democratic Party. Critics said he was too young, too inexperienced, too naive, too facile, too brash, and perhaps also too much in a hurry. He was, in the eyes of many, too much his father's son, and the father was widely feared and viewed as ruthless. He was also a Catholic. He was fiercely opposed by Harry Truman, Eleanor Roosevelt, Adlai Stevenson (who still harbored ideas of running for president himself), Senate Majority Leader Lyndon Johnson, Speaker of the House Sam Rayburn, and Senators Hubert Humphrey and Stuart Symington, to name just a few. Liberals questioned his lack of emotional commitment to their causes and wondered whether he was capable of exercising the moral leadership they demanded. When the going got rough they asked, would Kennedy stand up like Lincoln, Franklin Roosevelt, and Winston Churchill to fight for what was right? He had hardly impressed progressives back in 1954, for example: when the ultimate Joe McCarthy issue was raised, he was in a hospital bed and not in the Senate. Moreover, he never stated how he would have voted. He defended McCarthy in private, often noting that McCarthy was a good friend of his father and his family. Plainly, John Kennedy was worried about the strong McCarthy support among his Irish Catholic constituents, and he doubtless tried to duck the whole issue.

"I would hesitate to place the difficult decisions that the next president will have to make," said Eleanor Roosevelt, "with someone who understands what courage is and admires it, but has not quite the independence to have it."[12] Ironically, Kennedy later liked to quote Dante as saying the hottest places in hell "are reserved for those who, in a time of great moral crisis, maintain their neutrality." Still, Kennedy was forced to move somewhat to the left as he positioned himself for the 1960 nomination fight. He spoke increasingly of the Roosevelt legacy, and he tried, with some success, to rebuild the old New Deal coalition—the coalition that won the presidency in the 1930s and again in 1948 for Truman.

Kennedy ran against Eisenhower's record of slow action on education, civil rights, housing, urban problems, and the recession of the late 1950s. Had he run against President Eisenhower himself, Kennedy would have lost. Most anyone would have. Instead it was JFK's good fortune to run against Richard Nixon.

By 1960 Kennedy had become a talented, shrewd, and incandescent politician. His ability to speak to partisan and public crowds was impressive, and his ability to cut deals and orchestrate compromises with power brokers became refined. He had an appealing self-confidence, a considered optimism, and a refreshing idealism, and all this shone through. There is an old saying in politics that a candidate is greatly advantaged if he likes and enjoys people and even more if people know that he likes and enjoys them. Kennedy won praise in this regard. He liked himself, he liked politics, he liked and enjoyed people, and people knew it. He had stage presence and star quality.

He had another advantage. An old Kennedy family joke held that there are three things that help to win an election: "The first thing is money, the second thing is money, and the third thing is money." By 1960 Joe Kennedy was one of the wealthiest men in America, and it was several years before the coming of publicly financed presidential campaigns. Joe Kennedy probably gave more of his wealth to this election than any individual had ever given to a presidential candidate.

John Kennedy's political strategy in the 1960 campaign was clear. He would run against the complacency of the Republicans; hence, he ran to get things moving again. He ran to encourage economic growth. He ran to improve our national security and our standing in international affairs. He put Nixon on the defensive and appealed to those who believed America could be more productive at home and more of a world leader abroad. Throughout the campaign he portrayed himself as a leader, as an agent of revitalization, and as someone who would help America fulfill its true aspirations. In New York City, on October 27, 1960, Kennedy said: "I am sick as an American of reading these studies . . . which show that the image of America as a vital forceful society, as it once was under Franklin Roosevelt, has begun to fade. I believe it incumbent upon this generation of Americans to meet the same rendezvous with destiny of which Franklin Roosevelt spoke in 1936. This country has to do better. This country has to move again. This country has to provide full use of its people and all of its facilities if we are going to win out."[13]

And, later that same day in Sunnyside Gardens, Queens:

> Mr. Nixon and I disagree on what is the best interest of our country, and you have to make your judgment on November 8. . . . Mr. Nixon has run on a slogan that we have never had it so

> good. It indicates his belief that we are moving in a period now, to quote him, of "unparalleled prosperity," that the United States is moving in a position of strength and vitality, and that everything that must be done is being done in good measure. He looks around the world and he sees the United States with our prestige at an all-time high, and that of the Communists at an all-time low. I look at the world and I look at the United States, and I don't see his picture at all, and I am not, as the Democratic candidate for office, going to run for the Presidency in 1960, with any belief or any view that it is worthwhile getting elected President if we have to run on a platform which is totally unrealistic. This country is not moving ahead like it is going to have to move ahead if we are going to meet our responsibilities to ourselves, to those who come after us, to those who look to us around the world for leadership. And our position around the world is not unparalleled, our prestige has been higher. Our strength relative to the Communists has been greater. If Mr. Nixon hopes to be the President of the United States and present the United States to the world in the same image that he now presents it in this campaign, I could not disagree with him more. I hope you share the view with me that we want the truth with the bark off. The people of the United States want to face the facts. You share the same view that I do, that this country's potential is unlimited. There is no responsibility, no burden, no hazards that the United States cannot meet, but it certainly cannot meet those hazards unless the leadership is prepared to tell the truth.[14]

Nixon accused Kennedy of unpatriotically running down the nation, of lacking the necessary experience, and of advocating overly liberal programs that would bankrupt the treasury and inflate the cost of living.

What was Kennedy really saying? First, he was saying America had lost its way and it needed dynamic leadership again. Second, he was saying Nixon was wrong about our position in the world—perhaps also confused and deceptive. Finally, he appealed to patriotism and nationalism and summoned Americans to join in a crusade to make America the supreme leader in world affairs. Note, however, he rarely gave specifics. He would get the country moving again, but how he would do this was left open to the listener's imagination. The only new campaign idea to emerge was the Peace Corps, and even that had been incubating for a while in the Congress.

Kennedy had won the six primaries he entered that year by outcampaigning, outorganizing, and outspending Hubert Humphrey, his main challenger. His chief liabilities in the fall campaign would be his lack of executive experience and his Catholic faith.

Kennedy stressed time and again that he was not the Catholic candidate for president, but the Democratic Party's candidate for president who happened also to be Catholic. He noted that neither his deceased older brother nor he was ever questioned about their religion when they fought for the nation in World War II. "I do not speak for my Church on public matters—and the Church does not speak for me," he told a Baptist Convention in Houston. "If this election is decided on the basis of 45,000,000 Americans [losing] their chance of being President on the day they were baptized, then it is the whole nation that will be the loser in the eyes of history, and the eyes of our own people."[15]

In the debates with Vice President Nixon, Kennedy proved he could speak with just as much authority and knowledge about national security and economic policy matters. The debates plainly helped Kennedy display his leadership style, and this helped him to overcome what critics charged to be his chief liability, his lack of executive experience. His selection of Lyndon Johnson as his vice presidential running mate balanced the ticket by providing a regional and philosophical counterpoint to JFK. LBJ also played the elder statesman to Kennedy's youthful celebrity.

They won the election, yet it was one of the closest in American history. Kennedy won 49.7 percent of the popular vote, but he ran behind many of the House and Senate Democrats who were elected that year. He actually lost the majority of states. Democrats lost 20 seats in the House and 1 Senate seat. It was the first time in the twentieth century that a president's party failed to gain seats in Congress in a presidential election year. His margin in the electoral college was comfortable, 303 to 219, yet it is not entirely clear whether he or Nixon won the popular vote of the nearly 69 million who voted.[16] It was an inauspicious beginning.

Why did Kennedy win? No single factor explains it. President Eisenhower's limited and lukewarm efforts on behalf of Richard Nixon may have explained the difference. Lyndon B. Johnson helped in Texas and in a few other southern states. His father's money could have made the difference. The "it's time for a change" and "we can do better" themes helped. Mayor Richard Daley of Chicago may have helped in more ways than one. Kennedy's inspired and much appreciated phone call to the Martin Luther King family when Martin Luther King Jr. was in jail in Atlanta doubtless helped to attract black votes. His effectiveness in the first Kennedy-Nixon debate won him widespread attention and support. His youth, attractiveness, and charm, and effective campaign abilities were also factors, especially in a highly televised race. Political analysts believe it was less an issues election than it was an election based on partisanship and personality. Eisenhower Democrats came home that year. And Kennedy's personal style and star-quality attractiveness were critical factors.

When Kennedy came to office in early 1961, the United States was a nation of 180 million people. The national budget was slightly over $81 billion. Federal civilian employees numbered 2.3 million, and those in the military slightly over 1 million. Only 103 nations then existed. About 50 more nations would come into existence in the next 12 years. The Democrats controlled both houses in Congress, yet both houses were dominated by Southern Democrats.

Should Kennedy Have Been Elected President?

In retrospect there are at least some questions about John Kennedy that keep getting raised as to whether he should have been president.

The first is the question of whether Kennedy and his doctors lied about the seriousness of his physical fitness. He and his family were highly secretive about his adrenal insufficiency, or Addison's disease. Kennedy suffered from severe chronic back pain, a weakened spine, and a whole host of stomach and urinary ailments.

Kennedy lived with a variety of war injuries and inherited health problems. But as amazing as his stoicism was about his health challenges, it is now believed that if the facts of his health had been widely understood in 1959 or 1960 he doubtless would not have been nominated and elected president.[17]

His womanizing is yet another Kennedy habit or trait that, if it had been revealed, might have undermined his electability in 1960.[18]

His infidelities and male chauvinism were not broadly publicized at the time of his candidacy but are perhaps another aspect of his character that today at least would handicap his presidential aspirations. Note how even *Washington Post* owner Katherine Graham, a prominent partisan and social friend of JFK portrays him: "President Kennedy's charm was powerful. His intense concentration and gently teasing humor, and his habit of vacuum-cleaning your brain to see what you knew and thought, were irresistible. The Kennedy men were also unabashed chauvinists . . . they really didn't know how to relate to middle-aged women, in whom they didn't have a whole lot of interest."[19]

Katherine Graham adds a telling anecdote about how Kennedy wondered why it was that so many women liked Adlai Stevenson. A mutual friend told the president that while Stevenson and Kennedy both loved a lot of women, the big difference was that Stevenson liked women and women knew the difference. "They [women] all respond to a kind of message that comes across from Adlai when he talks to them. He conveys the idea that they are intelligent and worth listening to. He cares about what they're saying and what they've done." To which JFK responded: "Well, I don't say you're wrong, but I'm not sure I can go to those lengths."[20]

Finally, just about all the early histories or biographies of Kennedy by writers outside his personal loyalists depict him as an unusually restless, easily bored, and amazingly detached person. He had shown unusual braveness in World War II, and over the years he clearly developed a passion for competitive campaigning. But he seldom enjoyed strategic or philosophical planning. His campaigns were invariably run as personal, not party or ideological, initiatives. And his leadership efforts, if they can be called that, struck many people at the time, and later, as more transactional than transformative, more bystander than visionary.[21]

It is tempting to conclude, as many people do, that Kennedy's good looks and vast family wealth explain much of his political success. Yet his impressive war service, his 14 years of public service in Congress, his sophisticated grasp of professional and party politics, and his distinctive intellectual curiosity surely have to be credited as much for his successful pursuit of the presidency as his wealth, fame, and family.

What Kind of President?

Kennedy viewed the job of the president as one of helping to set the national agenda. His favorite presidents had been Jackson, Lincoln, and the Roosevelts. He also admired James Polk and Harry Truman for their determination and accomplishments. The presidency must be the center of moral leadership, a "bully pulpit," as Theodore Roosevelt explained it. He spent his first weeks recruiting his cabinet, staff, and advisers, wooing countless people of ability, especially university faculty and Rhodes Scholars to his administration. Proud of the talent and the energy of his new staff and cabinet, he also brought a few Republicans to top posts, yet he mostly appointed moderates to key positions. He was always somewhat nervous with liberals of the Americans for Democratic Action type. He went out of his way, with only an occasional exception, to select people who shared his pragmatic political views.

Kennedy was undeniably handsome and self-confident. He personified confidence, vitality, and pride in his own, and our, ability as a nation to get the job done. He disliked emotional scenes, clichés, and sentimental sappiness. His easy, spontaneous, and self-deprecatory humor won him great favor—especially with the press. He took his work seriously, but not himself. He could tell a joke, take a joke, and often joked about himself. And he loved political gossip. He also liked golf, at which he was good.

His supporters, such as historian Arthur M. Schlesinger Jr., saw him as a heroic and dashing figure: "The effortless charm, the high intelligence, the swift wit, the easy mastery at press conferences, the inspiring eloquence on the hustings. There was much more to him than that. He was a realistic politician, but he also had an exalted sense of America's responsibilities. He described himself as an 'idealist without illusions.' He was not satisfied with the way things were in America. His hope was to release resources of idealism he felt had been too long repressed in the national life."[22]

Kennedy believed the presidency was in the vital center of things. He believed Jeffersonian vision and Hamiltonian energy could make our complicated Madisonian system work to achieve Rooseveltian ends. His more favorable biographers have said that the inner confidence and competitive drive that Kennedy acquired as a youth freed him to grow as president, through one crisis after another. They say he grasped the full potentialities of the office.

Most analysts note, however, that Kennedy seemed to hold back, especially in pushing his domestic programs. Kennedy himself said that "great innovations should not be forced on slender majorities." Brookings Institution scholar James Sundquist explains the failure of Congress to enact the Kennedy program as chargeable to the simple fact that "the voters did not send Congress enough supporters of his program. His razor-thin popular majority was reflected in a Congress formally Democratic but actually narrowly balanced between activists and conservatives."[23] As often as not, it was the conservative faction of his own party that stymied progress.

In his inaugural address, Kennedy cautioned that policy changes would be difficult to achieve and slow in coming: "All this will not be finished in the first one hundred days. Nor will it be finished in the first one thousand days, nor in the life of this Administration, nor even perhaps in our lifetime on this planet. But let us begin." Several weeks later he quipped that the thing that surprised him most after he took office "was to find that things were just as bad as we'd been saying they were."[24]

His domestic program included aid to education (which was rejected), Medicare for the elderly (which was defeated), an urban cabinet department (which was rejected), and civil rights legislation (which he eventually pushed more vigorously, but which would not pass until after his death).

Kennedy critics portray him as having become even more conservative as president than he had been as a candidate. After having talked eloquently about the need for visionary leadership, in the White House he became cautious, pragmatic, and responsive primarily to what Congress and the American people would accept. Was this leadership? Or was it followership? Some faulted him for showing more profile than courage, for being more concerned with his Gallup poll ratings than with the moral ends for which the office should be used. "Kennedy had struggled to reach the top. Once there he paused, looked at the barriers to further progress, and rather than press forward accommodated himself to the realities," writes historian Herbert Parmet. "Where others may have seen opportunities, he found that the much advertised 'corridors of power' were really Byzantine labyrinths. His assessments argued for caution, for harnessing resources to fight the real battles some other day."[25]

The most positive view of the Kennedy presidency in domestic policy matters is as a period when the uncompleted domestic social policy agenda was consolidated and endorsed and left to incubate for the day when more progressives would be elected to the Congress. Kennedy at least sent the proposals and messages (dozens of them) to an unreceptive Congress, where the conservative coalition sat on them. Kennedy clearly identified with the needs of the elderly, the public schools, the cities, the minorities, and even women's rights, yet he only occasionally provided determined and forceful leadership on these issues. Later, both after Kennedy's death and after the decisive victories for progressive Democrats in 1964, Lyndon Johnson would gain acceptance for much of the Kennedy program. Thus, sympathetic analysts give Kennedy at least some of the credit for the successes of LBJ's Great Society.[26]

The most important domestic test for Kennedy was civil rights. He had been supportive of civil rights legislation as a senator, but he underestimated the moral passion behind the civil rights movement. It seemed at the time that he had never given it much thought. He would have to be educated, by events and by the movement.

Irish immigrants had been subjected to considerable discrimination, but Kennedy had little experience with that. Once in the White House he was cautious, perhaps even scared, of the civil rights issue. He was irritated when civil rights advocates confronted him and urged him to greater action. He appointed some segregationist judges in the South and delayed the executive order on housing that he had promised in his campaign; he could have made more black appointments. On the other hand, he appointed Thurgood Marshall to the federal bench, he opened the White House to blacks, and, through his brother Robert, he helped establish a working relationship between the Justice Department and the civil rights movement.

Students of the civil rights movement during the Kennedy years, such as Harris Wofford, Carl Brauer, and Nick Bryant, note that although Kennedy never encouraged blacks to march in the streets, he did foster an atmosphere in which protests against the status quo could occur. "His presidency marked a profound change from the inertia that had generally characterized the past," writes Brauer. "Kennedy both encouraged and responded to the aspirations of black Americans, and took his message to white Southerners."[27]

Still, Kennedy was often criticized for not caring enough, for never giving enough of himself, and for distancing himself from the civil rights ferment. Carl Stokes, the black mayor of Cleveland, never felt John Kennedy was a substantive man, that he was not in the same league as a Franklin Roosevelt or a Lyndon Johnson. "He used the liberal and minority groups but was never truly their friend." He suggests that the Kennedys understood the use of executive power outside their dealings with Congress. "They brought the steel industry to its knees and they used the Justice Department ruthlessly. In order to 'get' James Hoffa, they were as abrasive of the Constitution as any of the Watergate conspirators were. I have to believe that he understood how to deal with Congress," writes Stokes, "but he didn't care to pay the price for those things, and I take those things to be the things that mattered, the domestic issues."[28]

Reflections made by Martin Luther King Jr. are more positive. Reverend King viewed Kennedy as a sometime opponent and sometime friend. "The basic thing about him—he had the ability to respond to creative pressure," says King. "I never wanted—and I told him this—to be in the position that I couldn't criticize him if I thought he was wrong. And he said, 'It often helps me to be pushed.'" King added that when Kennedy saw the power of the movement, "he didn't stand there arguing about it. He had the vision and the wisdom to see the problem in all of its rich dimensions. And he had the courage to do something about it. He grew until the day of his assassination." "Historians will record that he vacillated like Lincoln," King believed, "but he lifted the cause far above the political level."[29] In an interview shortly after Kennedy's death, King said: "There were in fact two John Kennedys. One presided in the first two years under pressure of the uncertainty caused by his razor-thin margin of victory. In 1963, a new Kennedy had emerged. He had found that public opinion was not in a rigid mold. He was, at his death, undergoing a transformation from a hesitant leader with unsure goals to a strong figure with deeply appealing objective!"[30]

President Kennedy's record in foreign affairs was similarly marked by failures and by gradual improvement. This is not the place for a survey of his foreign policy record, but among the events that suggest a mixed performance are the Bay of Pigs, Laos, the Belgian Congo, Berlin, the Cuban Missile Crisis, the Nuclear Test Ban Treaty, the Alliance for Progress, the Peace Corps, and, of course, Vietnam. Progress, when it did come, came in fragments, accompanied by frustrations and setbacks. Kennedy was generally a "cold warrior" and a "hawk." This he had signaled in his campaign and in his earlier voting record. A more dovish Democrat could probably not have won election in 1960. Had he lived, Kennedy would have recognized some of his shortcomings in foreign policy, as his two brothers did, but he was the product of mainstream American thinking. "If Kennedy was a 'cold warrior,' who was not in his day? Who, that is, among those who could have plausibly risen to the presidency? He believed that strength was the most effective producer of reason, and that has yet to be disproved," writes Herbert Parmet in a balanced biography of Kennedy. "He saw the world as a dangerous place and reacted accordingly. If he had not, his inevitable replacement would have been someone who would have promised to really get tough."[31]

Kennedy's most remembered foreign policy statement came when he urged that the weapons of war must be abolished before they abolish us, and when he spoke as follows at American University in mid-1963:

> Today, should total war ever break out again—no matter how—our two countries would become the primary targets. It is an ironic but accurate fact that the two strongest powers are the two in the most danger of devastation. All we have built, all we have worked for, would be destroyed in the first twenty-four hours. And even in the Cold War, which brings burdens and dangers to so many countries, including this nation's closest allies our two countries bear the heaviest burdens. For we are both devoting to weapons massive sums of money that could be better devoted to combating ignorance, poverty, and disease. We are both caught up in a vicious and dangerous cycle in which suspicion on one side breeds suspicion on the other, and new weapons beget counterweapons.
>
> In short, both the United States and its allies, and the Soviet Union and its allies, have a mutually deep interest in a just and genuine peace and in halting the arms race. Agreements to this end are in the interests of the Soviet Union as well as ours—and even the most hostile nations can be relied upon to accept and keep those treaty obligations, and only those treaty obligations that are in their own interest. In the final analysis, our most basic common link is that we all inhabit this small planet. We all breathe the same air. We all cherish our children's future. And we are all mortal.[32]

The Kennedy Critics and Revisionists

As noted earlier, few presidencies have prompted both so many glowing biographers and so many harsh and stinging indictments. Because the glowing accounts are more well known and have shaped the Kennedy legend, let's look first at the critics. The Kennedy critics offer the following appraisals.

Garry Wills, in *The Kennedy Imprisonment* (1981), faults Kennedy for being preoccupied with sex, with a lust for power, and for giving us a presidency of appearances. He says Kennedy misunderstood the uses of power and in the end failed to learn, to teach, and to exercise moral leadership. Wills compares Kennedy with Martin Luther King Jr. and finds King's use of power "real" because it was not mere self-assertion or posturing. And King's work outlasted him. Unlike Kennedy, King changed the way Americans lived with each other. "The famous antitheses and alliterations of John Kennedy's rhetoric sound tinny now," writes Wills. "But King's eloquence endures, drawn as it was from ancient sources, the Bible, the spirituals, the hymns and folk songs. He was young at his death, younger than either Kennedy; but he had traveled farther."[33]

Richard Walton's provocative *Cold War and Counter Revolution* (1972) criticizes Kennedy for reckless military interventionism, for an unneeded military buildup, and for a brinksmanship that went beyond the maneuvering of Eisenhower's John Foster Dulles. Kennedy did not change the course of American history, writes Walton, but "pushed to its logical, tragic conclusion in Vietnam, the course begun by Harry Truman and carried on by Dwight Eisenhower. For Kennedy was not one to attempt to change America's sentiments, rather he was one to respond to its mood and exploit it. He moved back, not ahead as he promised."[34]

Journalist I. F. Stone spoke for the intellectual left when he wrote that abroad, as at home, the problems facing the nation were becoming too great for conventional leadership. But "Kennedy, when the tinsel was stripped away, was a conventional leader, no more than an enlightened conservative, cautious as an old man for all his youth, with a basic distrust of the people."[35] Similarly, iconoclastic British writer Henry Fairlie, in his *The Kennedy Promise* (1973), says Kennedy tried to govern and lead with rhetoric. He could summon the nation, yet he failed as a political coalition builder. "His triumph was one of style over substance. He confused popular leadership with political leadership. He turned us to foreign policy confrontations when he could not win any domestic policy victories here at home."[36] Former *New York Times* reporter and Pulitzer Prize–winning writer David Halberstam charged Kennedy, and all his well-educated advisers, with a failure to engage in critical thinking as the crisis in Vietnam escalated. Once committed, Halberstam claimed, their pride and reputations were on the line, and they could not admit their mistake.[37]

Nancy Gager Clinch, in her psychological "analysis" of Kennedy, contends that he sought power for his own inner needs more than from a desire to serve the nation. "I do not believe," she writes, "that Joseph Kennedy wanted political power for his sons because he wished to shape the nation's destiny. He lacked the social imagination for such an ambition. Rather, the evidence shows that the founding father's ambition was far simpler and narrower: to achieve a mammoth triumph over the prejudiced WASPs who had so often snubbed and despised him as the son of an Irish bartender."[38] She also writes that the "greatest tragedy of the Kennedy neurosis was that John Kennedy had qualities that aroused the hopes of the world for change and a better life, yet his own emotional shortcomings doomed these rekindled dreams to disappointment."[39]

Political scientist Bruce Miroff's *Pragmatic Illusions: The Presidential Politics of John F. Kennedy* (1976) faults Kennedy for failing to use his considerable gifts as an educator to rally the American people to various progressive causes. Kennedy never really trusted the American people or wanted a dialogue with them, Miroff contends, preferring to keep the people in the role of spectators. Miroff concludes that Kennedy's presidential record should serve as a warning to those who still believe that major changes in America can be instituted if the right liberal makes it into the White House. "Liberals will no doubt regain the Presidency in the future," he speculates. "But they will hardly refashion it into an instrument for the progressive transformation of American politics. That transformation can be accomplished only by those who have a stake in change. It is likely to be impeded by Presidents—who are, after all, the most successful products of the existing order."[40]

Thus, critics and revisionists conclude Kennedy was too often distracted by his own social life, perhaps lazy, and insufficiently willing to arouse the nation to the serious dilemmas of civil rights, tax reform, and women's rights. Candidate Kennedy had criticized President Eisenhower for indecisiveness, for lack of candor, for failure to use the full power of his office. Well, say critics, President Kennedy repeated most of these same weaknesses. During Kennedy's term, the voiceless remained generally voiceless, the poor remained poor, and the black and women's liberation movements, which had just begun, received only limited encouragement from Kennedy.

Kennedy's Legacy

Even Kennedy loyalist Arthur M. Schlesinger Jr., who served as a valued White House aide and later as the family historian, recorded in his personal journal his disappointment in JFK's timid rather than progressive leadership on economic issues. Here is a telling mid-1962 excerpt: "As I look back over the last year and a half, the main—and persisting—error of the

Kennedy administration has been the appeasement of business. This appeasement has been political and psychological rather than intellectual. . . . From the start, the President has shown an unfortunate disposition to consult those whom he regarded as enlightened and responsible business leaders . . . and make a special effort to meet their wishes. . . . At times he resents the process of appeasement and vents his resentment in private cracks about businessmen. But, when the chips are down, given the state of opinion in the Congress and in the country, he seems to feel no alternative but to pursue the appeasement line."[41]

John Kennedy, if he were with us, would agree with many of these criticisms, yet he would contend they are overdrawn. He would insist on being judged in the context of the political times in which he held office, he would stress the decidedly conservative outlook of the Congress and his slender election victory in 1960, and he would doubtless also note the limits of the presidency, enmeshed as it is in a relatively conservative, status-quo-preserving permanent bureaucracy.

He wanted to be remembered for making America more productive, more free, and more fair. His legacy lies less in what he achieved than in what he began. In his addresses in mid-1963 on civil rights, détente, and nuclear test ban matters, Kennedy was growing and maturing into a more sensitive, effective, and progressive national leader.

Kennedy also wanted to be remembered for "keeping the peace." He won credit for a mostly diplomatic solution to the Cuban Missile Crisis in 1962. He certainly earned credit as well for the 1963 nuclear test ban treaty. Yet he would probably agree with his secretary of defense, Robert S. McNamara, who later wrote that we underestimated the power of nationalism in Vietnam and we similarly failed to appreciate the limits of modern, high-technology military equipment.

McNamara emphasizes, and JFK would have agreed, that the fog of war clouds our rationality and we made a lot of mistakes in Vietnam.[42]

To dismiss John Kennedy as primarily a creature of style, however, is to miss much of the point of the American presidency. For, in addition to other responsibilities, a president is the custodian of American hopes, values, and dreams. Failure to fulfill this demand is at least as grievous—as Hoover and Carter learned—as failure in a president's other duties. John F. Kennedy was more than anything else a motivator, a morale builder, and a renewer of spirit.

Leadership, at its best, unlocks the talents and energies of the nation. In a time of turbulence, strong leadership provides a vision that helps empower all of us to rise above mere comportment to the status quo and make real contributions to our common purposes. Kennedy did many of these things well. He was genuinely popular and widely admired for his embodiment of the best in the national spirit. Those who overlook the forcefulness and the authenticity of his appeal misunderstand much of what he was about.

One of Kennedy's more lasting contributions was making public life attractive. He talked about politics and government, not as the problem, but as a means of solving problems. He got people involved. He made politics a worthy endeavor. He was able to inspire the nation, encourage the best in us, and appeal to our wellsprings of hope, compassion, and decency. The early 1960s marked a high point of American pride.

People felt proud of themselves and proud of their country. Trust in the national government was higher then than at anytime for the next two generations. Was this because of Kennedy or despite him? Probably both. Harris Wofford writes that Kennedy never expected to get all that he wanted, and he learned to live cheerfully—"perhaps too cheerfully—

with the continuing tension between what we know we are and what we ought to be."[43]

There would be later echoes of Kennedy's faith in politics and his optimism for the future of his country and how we could match our military and economic strength with moral initiatives, wisdom, and purpose. Ronald Reagan, Bill Clinton, and Barack Obama revisited these Kennedy themes—at least on occasion. And all three of them generously saluted JFK for his wit and especially his belief in the promise and possibilities of politics.

Political historian James MacGregor Burns offers this balanced verdict: "In the longer and broader judgment of history . . . he will be seen as a politician of extraordinary personal qualities who rhetorically summoned the American people to a moment of activism and greatness, who fell back on a conventional politics of brokerage, manipulation, and consensus once he attained office, who found the institutional constraints on action—especially in Congress—far more formidable than he had expected, who was intellectually too much committed to existing institutions to attempt to unfreeze them but lacked the passionate moral commitment necessary to try to transcend the restraints—and then, in his third year in the presidency and his last year on earth, he began to find his true direction and make a moral and political commitment to it."[44]

Kennedy, in his third year, did provide more aggressive leadership in civil rights, and he was able to gain Senate approval for a nuclear test ban treaty. He had also grown to realize, by 1963, that an antipoverty program should accompany his tax cuts. His friend and friendly biographer Arthur M. Schlesinger Jr. saw this third year as a turning point and that Kennedy had given America back to its better self, "wiping away the world's impressions of an old nation of old men, weary, played out, fearful of ideas, change and the future." Schlessinger adds, "The energies he released, the standards he set, the purposes he inspired, the goals he established would guide the land he loved for years to come."[45]

Part of the Kennedy paradox is that his presidency was one of both substance and myth. In his presidency, differing authors and analysts will readily find whatever they want to find. In his presidency we find much that is emblematic of the American people throughout our history: courage and caution, lightness and darkness, self-confidence and self-doubt, compassion and selfishness, integrity and occasional escapism. He was what we want to be and what we fear we sometimes are. He was both the product of his times, and he made them different. Like Kennedy's record, historians will forever be sorting out the myth from the reality of America itself.

Many have written of John Kennedy that his most notable achievement was the legend he left us. Myth, illusions, and dreams are very much part of the fabric of every tribe, every nation.

And the sudden end to Kennedy's presidency "left us with tantalizing 'might have beens,'" writes historian Robert Dallek. "Yet even setting these aside and acknowledging some missed opportunities and false steps," says Dallek, admiringly, "it must be acknowledged that the Kennedy thousand days spoke to the country's better angels, inspired visions of a less divisive nation and world, and demonstrated that America was still the last best hope of mankind."[46]

His thousand days was a much shortened presidency. It was as if Lincoln had died a few months after Gettysburg, or Franklin Roosevelt at the end of 1935, or Truman before the Marshall Plan. Despite his flaws and mistakes, Kennedy served to liberate and empower people to ask tough questions and dream of a better America. He had the effect of forcing people to rethink their values and develop new approaches. He had an impact on the bureaucracies of Washington, encouraging people to a higher level of imagination and to set higher standards of excellence than the standard operating procedure. If Kennedy were here today, he would remind us again that we can do better, that good people need to get involved, that the nation needs to get moving, and that America needs to earn respect throughout the world not only for its military and material successes but for living up to its constitutional ideals of liberty, equality, and social justice for all. He would reiterate that the task of the progressives is to represent the common man, that it is the glory and the greatness of our Jeffersonian and Rooseveltian tradition to speak for those who have no voice and to remember those who are forgotten and left behind.

Kennedy would urge us to be involved with the fights for economic growth and opportunity, for free and fair trade, for social justice, for educational opportunities for all, and for arms control as well as for an effective defense. Progress and justice come about because people and groups and movements organize, demand, push, and fight for their values, he would remind us. A president is hemmed in by the checks and balances and most especially by the well-organized privileged interests in the nation. The privileged interests, the political action groups, and the other Act III forces that strive to keep things as they are, need a counterweight, and he would urge Act I and Act II leaders to play that role. Above all, John Kennedy would urge all of us to take politics seriously and to understand that the nation needs not just a few "saviors" in high office, but thousands of citizen leaders in both the public and the private sector to make our system work.

Chapter Five
Problematic Presidential Power in Our Post-9/11 World

> The impact of 9/11 and of the ever-changing terrorist threat gives more power to the imperial presidency and places the separation of power ordained by the Constitution under unprecedented and at times unbearable strain.
>
> —Arthur M. Schlesinger Jr.[1]

The American presidency is a unique, necessary, and always potentially dangerous leadership institution. The framers of the U.S. Constitution knew this: They knew that if they invented a presidency with too much power, we risked ending up with an arbitrary tyrant, yet if they designed a presidency with too little power, the nation might not have the decisive leadership needed in time of emergency. Eleven generations later, we face the same questions the framers faced: What kind of president do we need? What kind of presidency do we want? How do we control an expansionist presidency in wartime? And granted that we need a powerful presidency, how do we prevent the type of autocratic leadership we fought the Revolution to rid ourselves of?

After the horrendous attacks of 9/11, President George W. Bush exhibited bold and consequential leadership. Yet with a retaliatory war in Afghanistan and a preventive war in Iraq, with the cost and duration of the occupation of Iraq unexpectedly growing, the controversial USA PATRIOT Act, several civil liberties controversies, increasing unilateralism at home and abroad, and the gnawing questions about motivation and honesty surrounding our Middle East policies, President George W. Bush and his administration challenged the constitutional system of checks and balances that are at the very heart of American democracy. Their argument, it is now clear, was that the United States could not win the war on terror without significantly expanding the powers of the presidency, even as this was done at the expense of Congress and civil liberties. Equally problematic was Bush's sweeping and now largely discredited nation-building initiative to democratize parts of the world that resist such conversion.[2]

The central question in this post–9/11 world is whether the new threat of Islamic fundamentalist terrorism set in motion a paradigm shift that renders our traditional means of defense obsolete, and whether it requires us to redefine the boundaries of executive power. At its heart, too, many of our initial responses have posed challenges to our ordinary interpretation of the U.S. Constitution.[3]

Is an eighteenth-century constitutional framework adequate or well suited to serve twenty-first-century needs? I shall argue here that it is and that the Bush administration heralds an unwelcome aberration from our cherished, yet still viable, tradition. Let's begin by exploring the development of executive power during wartime.

Executive Power during Wartime

Protection from attack—whether from external or internal threat—is a prime obligation for any nation. Thus it was that the American founders specified commander-in-chief authority when war is authorized. The framers explicitly gave Congress the responsibility to declare war, though they realistically expected presidents to repulse invasions and suppress insurrections.

Lincoln, Wilson, FDR, Truman, and several recent presidents have assumed broad executive powers as they sought to protect the nation's security. But the history of presidential use, and sometimes abuse, of the war power has become fraught with controversy. While some people applaud presidents for doing what had to be done, a number of scholars fear the U.S. Constitution has been incrementally eroded as president after president has redefined the war power as a primarily executive rather than constitutionally shared responsibility.[4]

The presumed lesson of the Japanese incarceration cases from the 1940s, the 1952 Harry Truman steel mills seizure, the Pentagon Papers fiasco, the Iran-Contra escapades in the 1980s, as well as many of Bush's post–9/11 actions, to be discussed, is that presidents are not above the law and cannot act unconstitutionally even in times of emergency. Further, at least a few judicial rulings in the George W. Bush era teach us anew that the Constitution is not what the president and his counselors say it is, and most assuredly a president "does not have unilateral and exclusive powers in all matters of national security."[5]

War has always nourished the possibility of an imperial presidency and the abuse of power. "War," James Madison famously said in 1795, "is the true nurse of executive aggrandizement." A president has no right, Madison insisted, to decide whether there is or is not cause of declaring war. "If Tyranny and Oppression come to this land," Madison said, "it will be in the guise of fighting a foreign enemy."[6] Almost every war and national emergency have tested our values and constitutional principles.

In a larger comparative context, wars invariably challenge any nation's existing checks and balances—even in nations with written constitutions and where personal rights are an entrenched part of society's customs. "Constitutional democracies have not succeeded in constructing a perfect system for controlling the state," writes historian Scott Gordon, "and like other dimensions of social perfection, such an ideal is unlikely to come within our grasp. But while perfection is impossible, improvement is not."[7]

The attacks of September 11, 2001, transformed the George W. Bush presidency and led to two wars, the PATRIOT Act, the creation of a 180,000-person Homeland Security Department, and a variety of constitutional clashes in the courts and elsewhere. George W. Bush boldly justified strengthened presidential war-making and related emergency powers. Bush consciously assumed fellow Republicans Teddy Roosevelt's and Ronald Reagan's view of a vigorously assertive presidency. But he went beyond them, repeatedly arguing that the law and the Constitution must adjust to the necessity born of this new age of terrorism. Bush set new records for presidential usurpation of powers.

By claiming an exclusive presidential power of declaring preventive war and by denying U.S. citizens as well as foreign suspects a host of civil liberties routinely assured in the United States, and by practicing unprecedented use of "extraordinary rendition" programs and questionable interrogation procedures, Bush seemed to many observers to be acting outside of the Constitution and our Bill of Rights.[8]

There is agreement now that the post–9/11 roundup of illegal immigrants was excessive and, in some cases, violated the rights of innocent individuals. The Bush administration has also been accused of abducting suspects here and abroad and deporting them to other nations where they can be imprisoned or tortured as part of interrogation (the so-called policy of extraordinary rendition).[9]

"The use of military force by President George W. Bush against Iraq poses a threat to constitutional government, civil liberties and national security," says political scientist Louis Fisher. "It represents the culmination over the past 50 years of unilateral presidential wars accompanied by few checks from Congress or the judiciary."[10]

The American framers rejected the notion of presidents initiating war. Their sense of history, as Louis Fisher reminds us, held that executives often commenced wars more for personal, political, partisan, or even family reasons than they did for valid reasons of national interest.

The American framers plainly took a narrow view of the commander-in-chief authority. Years later, Abraham Lincoln, while serving in Congress, cautioned his countrymen that the Philadelphia Convention had resolved to so frame the Constitution that no one man should hold the power of bringing the oppression of war upon us.

Yet in recent generations the American people and the Congress have placed enormous amounts of military power in the hands of their presidents. The Iraq war, critics now agree, has resurrected the imperial presidency once associated with LBJ and Richard Nixon, and with it came a cavalier disrespect for individual freedoms and due process. Historian Arthur M. Schlesinger Jr., writing in the middle of the George W. Bush years, concluded that the contemporary presidency, sadly, "has come to see itself in messianic terms as the appointed savior of a world whose unpredictable dangers call for rapid and incessant deployment of men, arms, and decisions behind a wall of secrecy." He adds, "This view seems hard to reconcile with the American Constitution."[11]

The United States now has troops at hundreds of military bases in nearly 60 nations, and in George W. Bush it has a president who has deep suspicions of international law, serious reservations about the Geneva Conventions, and implicit, if not explicit, contempt for the United Nations. Bush's ambassador to the United Nations openly stated his belief, for example, that international law is not binding, merely a temporary diplomatic convenience.[12] The Bush-Cheney era has been so committed to protecting and enlarging presidential power that its unilateralism and go-it-alone approach has, ironically, weakened the presidency. It is in many important ways the antithesis of how Lincoln and Roosevelt operated. "The Bush administration has operated on an entirely different concept of power that relies on minimal deliberation, unilateral action, and legislative defense," writes Harvard law professor and former Bush Justice Department counsel Jack Goldsmith. "This approach largely eschews politics: the need to explain, to justify, to convince to get people on board, to compromise."[13]

Presidential scholars are virtually in agreement that presidents who use and stretch their "hard" formal powers but neglect their informal "softer" powers of persuasion and education will likely lose both the Congress and the people. And this is exactly what has happened with the Bush presidency and its power grabs and failed efforts at educating and convincing the American people. The lesson here is clear: You cannot win the respect and trust of Congress and the American people if you lie to them, engage in unprecedented secrecy, and bypass cherished principles of constitutionalism.[14]

George W. Bush was not the only president who relished clashes with Congress and the courts. Presidents and the Congress regularly try to reassert their authority. FDR, Harry Truman, LBJ, Reagan, and Bill Clinton all stretched the legal limits of their office.[15]

Writers on the American presidency regularly note that we need Hamiltonian energy in the presidency to make our Madisonian system of separation of powers work, in order to advance the Jeffersonian, Lincolnian, and Rooseveltian goals of freedom, liberty, justice, and equality.[16] But an energetic presidency is far different from an imperial presidency.

Some writers contend, too, that grave emergencies require the bending of constitutional restrictions on an American president. In times of national security crises, a constitutional democracy must be temporarily altered to what is necessary, writes historian Clinton Rossiter. Once the peril has been overcome, normal practices are restored. Rossiter wrote in the shadow of World War II and the Korean War, and his conclusion was: "We must cease wasting our energies in discussing whether the government of the United States is to be powerful or not. It is going to be powerful or we are going to be obliterated. Our problem is to make that power effective and responsible, to make any future dictatorship a constitutional one. No sacrifice is too great for our democracy, least of all the temporary sacrifice of democracy itself."[17]

Rossiter, in the 1950s, and much later, several George W. Bush advisers concluded that Congress's size, disunity, slowness, and unwillingness to take political risks forced it into playing at best a secondary leadership role in national security matters. Bush advisers, such as John Yoo, argued that the framers of the U.S. Constitution would, if they were alive today, understand "a commander in chief as having authority over when to resort to military hostilities and how to conduct them."[18] This Bush legal adviser goes on to say that his reading of the Constitution gives a president both the authority and the responsibility for preventing future attacks against the United States—and thus implicitly if not explicitly—presidents have the authority to initiate preventive wars.[19]

"Like any brittle thing, a Constitution that will not bend will break," adds influential federal judge Richard A. Posner.[20] Posner posits that national survival and the safety of the people are the supreme laws that necessarily guide presidents. Thus he is little troubled by most of the measures taken after the 9/11 attacks save for the Bush administration's wrong-minded "effort to deny the right of habeas corpus to U.S. citizens—a measure that the Supreme Court invalidated—and to foreign terrorist suspects captured in the United Sates."[21]

Yet neither the president nor Congress is always right. "That is why the Constitution provides for 'joint possession' and enjoins partnership," writes Arthur M. Schlesinger Jr. "Congress must recognize that it cannot conduct day-to-day foreign relations. The president must understand that no foreign policy can last that is not founded on popular understanding and congressional consent." Schlesinger cautions, however, that "it would be a mistake to surrender to a romantic view of the superior wisdom of Congress. The legislative branch can be just as wrongheaded, impulsive, emotional, gullible, and dishonorable as the executive. . . . Sometimes presidents are wiser and better informed; sometimes they aren't."[22]

The genius of republican liberty and our constitutional processes is that the partnership of president and Congress—sometimes in collaboration, sometimes in creative tension—will help produce prudent policies. Our constitutional framers justly celebrated the political independence of our governmental branches and separation of powers as a device to constrain as well as restrain the power of the central government by enabling each of the federal branches to negate acts of the others. The prevention of tyranny was the goal. Shared and intermixed powers were a central means to this end.

Each incumbent president understandably defines and exploits, up to a point, the formal and latent authority, or hard power, that exists in the modern-day presidency. Circumstances, personality, the nature of the times, public expectations, as well as which party controls Congress, all play a role in how presidents exercise leadership.

Presidents have to live with the abiding ambivalence most Americans have toward power and governmental leadership. We want leadership, yet we also want to be free. We admire the purposeful use of power, yet we fear it may be abused if not adequately checked. And we doubtless love our country and its heritage of liberty, yet we have never particularly liked government itself; and we are especially frustrated by the constant bickering that takes place between Congress and the White House, and between the two major parties.

In the aftermath of 9/11, Americans welcomed assertive and authoritative antiterrorism presidential activism. Yet as time passed, and mistakes and excesses became understood, when $2 trillion or more was spent on various war initiatives and overseas nation-building, 10 times more than top Bush officials had earlier forecast, even some of those who supported President Bush became frustrated if not outright critical of his judgment and presidential leadership. Bush plainly responded, perhaps overresponded to American wishes for strength, protection, and even revenge. Eventually, however, Americans also made it clear they wanted honesty, explanation, admission of mistakes, and wanted the White House to adhere—at least in broad terms—to the accepted guidelines of constitutional restraint.

Thus, George Bush belatedly learned, Americans simultaneously wanted firm, forceful presidential leadership that would prevent terrorist attacks on our homeland, but also feared a president who acted alone, isolated America, and often sounded too self-assured.

The following list of developments in the George W. Bush presidency justifiably raised concern:

- The claim that a president has the right to initiate preventive war
- The claim that the president has sole authority to designate individuals as enemy combatants and how, where, and when they would be tried[23]
- Executive branch suspension of habeas corpus rights[24]
- Overzealous roundup of illegal aliens
- Misuse and mismanagement of intelligence agencies[25]
- Prisoner abuse at Abu Ghraib, Guantánamo, and elsewhere, and secretly run CIA-operated prisons in several undisclosed foreign nations
- Disregard for the United Nations and international law
- A Bush administration advisory memorandum, later disavowed, that argues for a narrow definition of torture and held that in deciding how to treat detainees, a president is bound neither by domestic nor international law or agreements[26]
- Excessive and illegal "extraordinary rendition" polities (the program of arresting alleged terrorists in one country and shipping them off to yet another country for interrogation and possibly torture)
- Unilateralism in foreign affairs and strained relations with traditional allies

- Discouragement of dissent and debate about the validity of war initiatives
- Dubious use of bill-signing statements as at least an implicit means of encouraging agencies to disobey laws[27]
- Executive branch subsidies and commissions for supportive cheerleading members of the press
- White House leaks about a CIA operative
- Politicizing the Justice Department's prosecutors
- Providing no-bid war contracts to administration-friendly companies
- Vice President Cheney's refusal to release public information relating to his office's activities—in part alleging that his is a legislative, not an executive, position

The overall pattern raises both perennial questions about the presidency and constitutionalism, as well as new questions shaped by twenty-first-century realities.

First, some of the enduring questions about the presidency and constitutionalism:

1. Is the war-making authority of the U.S. Congress now all but irrelevant and discarded?
2. Does it have to be that we have one Constitution for peacetime and yet another for times of war or in times of permanent terrorist threat?
3. Can't we balance stalwart patriotism with the right to question the policies of a wartime president—during election years and in between?
4. What are the valid and necessary sources of American legitimacy in international relations?

5. Both conservative and liberal advocates of a stronger Hamiltonian presidency have long held that Congress and the courts sometimes need to permit greater leeway to presidents than may be explicitly spelled out either in the Constitution or in the law. If so, should we amend the Constitution and rewrite the laws to reflect this, or wholly ignore constitutional prescriptions? Or, alternatively, is there a way we can insist that Congress and future presidents abide by our constitutional guidelines?

Here are newer questions, sharpened by recent developments:

1. What is the constitutional legitimacy of the doctrine of preventive war?
2. What conditions must be met, if any, for such a war to be launched?
3. Does a president have the authority to imprison individuals as enemy combatants just by declaring such without due process and judicial review?
4. What is the proper role for the federal courts and the Congress in a post–9/11 era?
5. Can a president in the commander-in-chief role merely bypass U.S. laws and international treaties that prohibit inhumane treatment of prisoners?
6. Is there a new paranoia (akin to McCarthyism) shaping the PATRIOT Act, the Homeland Security Department, treatment of suspects, and our apparent disrespect for privacy rights of our own citizens?
7. What constitutes legitimate military or humanitarian intervention in the twenty-first century? Iraq,

Darfur, Rwanda, Kosovo? How and why do we decide to stand aside, intervene, and when to act?

8. What is our position in the international community and in the United Nations if we choose to act unilaterally?
9. What is the desirable interpretation of the Geneva Conventions?
10. What effect will a near-constant state of war abroad have upon our democratic traditions and institutions at home?

The importance of these questions is heightened by several new realities:

- The United Nations, which was designed to be weak, is in fact exceptionally weak and slow to react to international crises.
- Americans are painfully divided about what role the United States should play in humanitarian and world-policing activities.
- While America has several new economic and political rivals, it continues to spend more on defense than most of the rest of nations combined.
- Clashing cultures or civilizations and ethnic conflicts, which have always existed, have more than replaced the tensions of the long Cold War.
- The world, at least in the Bush years, lost faith in America's intentions and example.

Conservative supporters of President George W. Bush view the United Nations as irrelevant and hold that only the United States could stand up to the Taliban, Saddam Hussein, North Korea, Iran, and whoever else threatens U.S. security interests. We have to act, they say, because if we didn't, we would be virtually inviting more terrorist attacks and possibly even nuclear, chemical, and biological attacks from these new enemies. They add: covert operations by the CIA, extraordinary rendition policies, and severe interrogation techniques are a necessity of war, and if they succeed in preventing terrorist attacks on American soil, these policies justify themselves by saving hundreds of thousands of American lives. This is a message that won initial approval from Congress, from the American people, and from putatively liberal leaders such as Tony Blair and Hillary Clinton, and seemed to be validated in the presidential and congressional election results of 2004. This proved less so in the midterm elections of 2006, where Bush supporters lost significant ground, and where, had his name been on the ballot, Bush himself probably would have lost his election.

Still, many Americans are also uneasy about the emergence of what may be described as an American empire and are worried about the costs in terms of human life, treasure, and freedoms enumerated in the Bill of Rights. New York University professor Tony Judt may be correct when he argues that "[i]n the longer run no country can expect to behave imperially—brutally, contemptuously, illegally—abroad while preserving republican values at home. For it is a mistake to suppose that institutions alone will save a republic from the abuses of power to which empire inevitably leads. It is not institutions that make or break republics, it is men. And in the United States today, the men (and women) of the country's political class have failed. Congress appears helpless to impede the concentration of power in the executive branch; indeed, with few exceptions it has contributed actively and even enthusiastically to the process."[28]

Bush's credibility was diminished when he first justified the Iraq campaign with weapons of mass destruction (which never appeared), then with the assertion that the 9/11 terrorists had strong ties to Saddam Hussein (which didn't prove true), then with the notion that Iraq had the intention to make WMDs (also not significantly proven), and finally with the idea that the world will be safer if we can bring democracy to the Middle East (which might be the case but is now a largely discredited transformational project). All but gone was any rationale that legitimized our preventive war in the first place.

Further, Bush seriously underestimated the Sunni resistance to the U.S. occupation of Iraq and exaggerated our successes ("mission accomplished") and costs in terms of lives, money, and political support while mindlessly, or perhaps shamelessly, overestimating the role Iraq's oil industry might play in rebuilding Iraq's infrastructure.[29] Suddenly we became engaged in nation-building with inadequate planning, in a nation where many, if not most, of its citizens, did not especially want us there as a nation-builder.[30]

The "Unitary Executive" Theory

A so-called unitary executive or unitary presidency theory began to be developed in the Ronald Reagan years, which described White House efforts to oppose congressional initiatives that sought to bypass presidential control of agency regulations. These had mostly to do with domestic public policy matters. A few aides to George H. W. Bush also propounded a "unitary presidency" theme, warning administration lawyers to be wary of any congressional encroachment on presidential prerogatives.

Bill Clinton and his advisers did not employ the term. As has been documented, however, Clinton on a few occasions chose to engage in selective military ventures abroad without formally consulting the Congress (and in one notable case in defiance of Congress).

But in George W. Bush's first term, well after 9/11 and our initial responses to those attacks, this unitary presidency theory was regularly relied upon to describe the Bush-Cheney claim that Congress cannot limit or regulate how a president exercises the commander-in-chief responsibilities, especially the way we go to war, target and detain terrorists, and whether or not we torture or employ "enhanced interrogation" techniques against prisoners of war in this new age of terrorism.

This ever-more-capacious usage of the unitary executive doctrine raised a lot of issues. The Bush-Cheney interpretation that gained prominence in 2004 signaled an expansive theory of presidential authority and claimed that legislative encroachments of any kind on a president's authority to direct the actions of the executive branch or its employees are a violation of our separation-of-powers doctrine and thus unconstitutional.

Here are two examples: According to the Bush administration, the president has the right to initiate preventive wars with or without congressional authorization. Moreover, Bush, in effect, said that his commander-in-chief role allows him to ignore most acts of Congress, save budgetary restrictions, that seek to regulate the military and his conduct of war.

Second, in the words of a White House signing statement detailing how Bush (and presumably Cheney) construed the 2005 Detainee Treatment Act's restrictions on interrogation power as unacceptable, "the White House" would interpret it "in a manner consistent with the constitutional authority of the President to supervise the unitary executive branch and as Commander in Chief and consistent with the constitutional limitations on the judiciary power, which will assist the shared objectives of the Congress and the President . . . of protecting the American people from further terrorist attacks."[31]

In effect Bush was saying that he was "the decider," that is, as various emergencies or circumstances arose, he—and not the Congress or the courts—would make the critical decision about preventive wars as well as what interrogation methods were warranted. In short, Bush declared that the ultimate and seemingly exclusive war-making authority rested with his office.

Here is how political scientist David Gray Adler summarizes what he believes is both the unconstitutional and out-of-control "unitary executive" model: "The president … may initiate preventive war without authorization from Congress[;] . . . he has the sole and exclusive authority to conduct war. Congressional directions and instructions are invidious . . . and represent an encroachment on presidential power. . . . Statutes in conflict with the president's policies represent a violation of executive authority. It is contended that the president may designate, seize, and detain any American citizen as an 'enemy combatant' and imprison him in solitary confinement, indefinitely, without access to legal counsel and a judicial hearing. . . . Under this theory, any law that restricts the Commander in Chief's authority is presumptively unconstitutional. At all events, the president may exercise an 'override' authority in the unlikely event that Congress would by statute seek to restrain the president."[32]

Pulitzer Prize–winning journalist Charlie Savage cataloged the Bush-Cheney presidentialist credo and its considerable success in expanding presidential powers at the expense of Congress and the courts. The White House political control over the executive branch, Savage contends, was dramatically expanded. The White House often claimed the power to bypass laws it believed would handicap their antiterrorist efforts. And the explosive use of bill-signing statements is, Savage adds, "a dramatic change that has the potential to take away from Congress its constitutional right to override a president's decision to reject a new law."[33]

Historically, when a president signed a bill enacted by Congress, he issued a signing statement indicating reasons for supporting the legislation. In the 1980s Ronald Reagan occasionally indicated in his statements how federal agencies should interpret and administer the new laws in different ways from what Congress may have intended. George W. Bush seized upon this procedure and in well over a thousand cases indicated his own interpretation of a bill or certain sections of a bill. In Bush's use the signing statement came close to becoming an item veto.

The tortured logic of the unitary presidency theory is that eventually a president becomes unaccountable and imperial—and our aspirations as a constitutionally representative and deliberative democracy are irretrievably diminished.

Precedent after precedent point in the direction of a presidency-dominated decisionmaking system. "The importance of such precedents is difficult to overstate," writes Savage, who concludes his study by quoting Supreme Court justice Robert Jackson, who had warned that bold new claims of presidential power, once validated as precedents, are a lot "like a loaded weapon ready for the hand of any authority that can bring forward a plausible claim of an urgent need. Every repetition imbeds that principle more deeply in our law and thinking and expands it to new purposes."[34]

Bush eventually lost a few court cases in the federal district courts, as well as at the Supreme Court. At one point, one of his own Republican appointees to the federal court, U.S. Judge Henry F. Floyd of South Carolina, felt compelled to write that "the court finds that the President has no power, neither express nor implied, neither constitutional nor statutory, to hold petitioners as an enemy combatant. [if he did it] would not only affect the rule of law and violate this country's traditions, but it would also be a betrayal of this nation's commitment to the separation of powers that safeguards our democratic values and individual liberties." Floyd found Bush lacked the authority to hold Jose Padilla, a U.S. citizen arrested in Chicago on suspicion of terrorism in May 2002, in indefinite military custody. "Simply stated," Floyd wrote, "this is a law enforcement matter, not a military matter."[35] Floyd was later overruled by an appeals circuit judge, yet controversy on this issue continued.

Similarly the Supreme Court ruled in 2004 that foreign prisoners held at Guantánamo Bay have the constitutional right to contest their detentions in a federal court. In effect, the court, in a series of rulings, held that the Bush administration needed to provide due process for detainees and so-called enemy combatants. The very notion of a president having the authority to indefinitely incarcerate American citizens or foreign-born nationals without charge, without access to counsel, and without judicial review struck many judges as well as many Americans as arbitrary and dangerous. Most people believed along with Justice Sandra Day O'Connor that Bush's undeclared state of war was not a blank check for the president when it comes to the rights of the nation's citizens.[36]

The Geneva Conventions protect U.S. military personnel when they are captured, and thus the Bush administration's reluctance to comply with it when we captured our enemies upset many people, including U.S. military leaders and conservative U.S. senators.[37] Senator John McCain and others added an amendment in 2005 to a defense bill requiring the U.S. military to abide by the Geneva Convention that prohibits "cruel, inhumane or degrading" treatment in prisoner interrogations. President George W. Bush opposed this amendment, yet later grudgingly signed the bill into law. Bush, though publicly saying that "this government does not torture and that we adhere to the international convention of torture," issued one of his famous signing statements stipulating that this McCain provision might violate his commander-in-chief powers and that he might in the future not necessarily act in compliance with it. "The only thing achieved by the statement," said one former Bush appointee, "was to spoil the tentative consensus and goodwill that had been reached with Capitol Hill on the issue, and further enflame mistrust of the President."[38]

Many Americans were also upset by the failure of the Bush administration to accept responsibility and accountability for the inappropriate prisoner abuses at Abu Ghraib. "The Abu Ghraib photographs and subsequent detailing of wrongdoing by military and civilian interrogators and guards at Guantánamo and in Iraq and Afghanistan," said the *Los Angeles Times*, "are among the most shameful chapters in this war on terror."[39] Joseph Galloway, senior military correspondent for the Knight Ridder (now McClatchy) newspapers, added, "It's long past time for responsibility to begin flowing uphill in this administration. . . . Now is the time to state plainly and unequivocally that we are Americans and we live by a rule of law that protects everyone, even the worst terrorist who ever fell into our hands."[40]

So the question remains: What kind of a presidency do we need and want for the rest of the twenty-first century? Right-leaning and left-leaning advocates will differ, yet it is in everyone's interest to want to restore America's legitimacy as an agent for international peace and prosperity. All of us want to strengthen constitutional practices and the rights and liberties so elegantly laid out in our Bill of Rights. And, most assuredly, all of us want to prevent both nuclear war and terrorism.

These aspirations are as challenging as they are worthy. But they are absolutely worth debating against the practicalities of today's new realities. Freedom and liberty cannot be spread by the military alone. Other, more useful, means of success in our war on terror are available. Understanding of one another's cultures is as important today as economic development. A strengthened and more creative United Nations, World Bank, and transnational processes are essential. Greater investments in trade, in sensible immigration policy, and in research and technology will go a long way toward sustaining and building upon U.S. international leadership.[41]

More realistic foreign aid strategies are needed. The role of the Peace Corps and international agreements such as the Geneva Conventions have to be taken more seriously—even if they have to be modified or adapted to new realities.

"The years when the United States appeared as the hope of the world now seem long distant," write international affairs scholars Robert Tucker and David Hendrickson. "Washington is hobbled by a reputation for the reckless use of force and it is going to take a long time to live that down. World public opinion now sees the United States increasingly as an outlier—invoking international law when convenient, and ignoring it when not; using international institutions when they work to its advantage, and disdaining them when they pose obstacles to U.S. design."[42]

We should never underestimate, too, the role human rights and moral authority must play in our foreign policy. Ancient empires engaged in torture and brutality without losing their legitimacy. But the United States cannot. Yale

Law School professor Amy Chua elaborates: "American power in the twenty-first century depends on whether the United States can be the nation that my parents and many millions of other immigrants came to know: a country that stood for both strength and decency. If we lose that moral authority, America's global dominance will be rejected by the billions of non-Americans over whom the United States projects its power. America's ability to lead, let along inspire, will be severely compromised. And in an increasingly competitive world economy, the most talented and skilled immigrants will look elsewhere, eroding the formula for America's remarkable success that has worked for two centuries."[43]

We need also to appreciate the paradoxes of American presidential leadership. We want visionary leadership, yet not dogmatism. We want self-confidence and decisiveness, yet we are inherently and justifiably suspicious of leaders who appear to act unilaterally and do not persuade Congress and the nation as to the proper course of action. We want a president who will work with Congress and the opposition party, listen as well as lead, and be reflective as well as decisive.

We need to celebrate politics and political discourse. We need to encourage debate and healthy dissent. A "truly strong president," Arthur M. Schlesinger Jr. reminded us, "is not the one who relies on power to command but the one who recognizes his responsibility, and opportunity, to enlighten and persuade."[44]

Imagine the qualities and character of a president and a presidency that might heal the ill will toward the United States and much of our recent foreign policy. Imagine pragmatic coalition-building, yet unifying leadership that can help reclaim America's role as the hope of those everywhere who dream of liberty, justice, and constitutional democracy:

- Imagine a president who will defend American sovereignty, yet work to restructure as well as strengthen the United Nations as a more effective peacekeeping force.[45]
- Imagine a president who will reach out to both traditional and new allies to contain nuclear proliferation and combat terrorism.
- Imagine a president who recognizes the importance of generally accepted international law and agreements such as the Geneva Conventions, and who will work to fashion new approaches toward world peace and civility.
- Imagine a president who welcomes real debate about foreign policy, and who would agree with the late U.S. senator Bob Taft of Ohio when he said in 1941 that "there can be no doubt that criticism in time of war is essential to the maintenance of any kind of American government."[46]
- Imagine a president who understands constitutionalism, and who recognizes the real partnership Congress must play in shaping national security and foreign policy and in deciding about going to war.[47]
- Imagine a president who strengthens our democratic goals of justice and equality on the domestic front at the same time he or she argues for the possibilities of freedom and democracy abroad.
- Imagine a president who can admit mistakes and reverse course if it is the right thing to do for the national interest.
- Imagine a president who condemns abuses of the Abu Ghraibs, whether run by the Saddam Husseins, the United States, or anyone else.

- Imagine a president who sides with U.S. general David Petraeus, a recent Iraq commander, who instructed his troops that "some may argue that we would be more effective if we sanctioned torture or other expedient methods of obtaining information from the enemy. . . . They would be wrong. Beyond the basic fact that such actions are illegal, history shows that they also are frequently neither useful nor necessary."[48]
- Imagine a president who understands the famous 1866 court ruling (*Ex Parte Milligan*) that "the Constitution is a law for rulers and people, equally in war and in peace, and covers with the shield of its protection all classes of men, at all times, and under all circumstances,"[49] and the 2008 ruling in *Boumediene v. Bush* that, in Justice Anthony Kennedy's majority opinion, "The laws and Constitution are designed to survive, and remain in force, in extraordinary times."[50]
- Imagine a president who fashions a serious and sustained long-term policy of energy security and aggressively invests in renewable energy alternatives and serious energy conservation.
- Imagine a president who becomes a world leader on issues of genocide, malaria, AIDS, land mines, poverty, and global warming.
- Imagine a president who acts by example, as Justice Louis Brandeis imagined when he wrote: "our government is the potent, the omnipresent teacher . . . it teaches the whole people by its example—if the government becomes a lawbreaker, it breeds contempt for the law, it invites every man to become a law unto himself."[51]

Yes, this is a lot to imagine, but we often pay a high price for not imagining a better and more appropriately constitutional presidency. Similarly, we pay a high price when the Congress fails to exercise its appropriate constitutional checks and balances. We must remember the warning of Justice Robert Jackson when he wrote, "We may say that power to legislate for emergencies belongs in the hands of Congress, but only Congress itself can prevent power from slipping through its fingers."[52]

The Bush administration declined to designate the Guantánamo detainees as prisoners of war, and held many of them for up to six years without filing charges against them or allowing them counsel. "That is shameful, not at all the way an American government devoted to protecting liberty should operate," editorialized my libertarian-leaning local newspaper. "What distinguishes the United States and other civilized countries from the barbaric terrorists who seek to harm us is precisely our devotion to the rule of law and orderly procedures."[53]

The American presidency has changed not only because of 9/11, but also because of an ever-changing and highly complicated balance of powers, nuclear proliferation, new technologies, and the rise of new industrial and information-age giants such as China and India. We need today a sustained debate about the kind of presidency we want, a debate that acknowledges both the new realities of the twenty-first century and the enduring values of liberty, justice, and countervailance that have shaped our constitutional republic. Surely, too, we can refashion a relationship between Congress and the presidency that can appropriately support a president's responsible efforts to enhance our national security yet also appropriately constrain and keep presidents accountable.[54]

Notes

Chapter 1

1. Jonathan Alter, "The Obama Dividend," *Newsweek*, March 31, 2008, p. 37.

2. Alexander Hamilton, *Federalist, No. 68*, in Alexander Hamilton, John Jay, and James Madison, *The Federalist* (New York: The Modern Library, 1937), p. 444.

3. Madison, *Federalist, No. 10*, ibid., p. 57.

4. See Joseph J. Ellis, "When a Saint Becomes a Sinner," *U.S. News and World Report*, November 9, 1998, p. 67.

5. Bradley, quoted in "Rules of the Game," *New York Times Magazine,* March 25, 2007, p. 15.

6. Alter, "The Obama Dividend," p. 37.

7. See, for example, Gary Jacobson, *A Divider Not a Uniter* (New York: Pearson, 2007).

8. See, for example, Alexander Pelosi, *Sneaking into the Flying Circus: How the Media Turn Our Presidential Campaigns into Freakshows* (New York: Free Press, 2005).

9. I have written about these paradoxes of the presidency in Thomas E. Cronin and Michael A. Genovese, *The Paradoxes of the American Presidency* (New York: Oxford University Press, 2004), ch. 1.

10. See the excellent books by James P. Pfiffner, *The Character Factor: How We Judge America's Presidents* (College Station: Texas A&M University Press, 2004), and Joanne B. Ciulla, ed., *Ethics: The Heart of Leadership* (Westport, CT: Praeger, 1998).

11. Quoted in Richard L. Berke, "In Presidents, Virtue Can Be Flaws (and Vice Versa)," *New York Times*, September 27, 1998, sec. 4, p. 1.

12. Ted Sorensen, *Counselor* (New York: HarperCollins, 2008), p. 123.

13. Michael Walzer, *Thinking Politically* (New Haven, CT: Yale University Press, 2007), p. 302. See also his "The Problem of Dirty Hands," ibid., pp. 278–295.

14. I have borrowed here from Thomas E. Cronin and Michael A. Genovese, "President Clinton and Character Questions," *Presidential Studies Quarterly* (Fall 1998): 892–897. See, too, the excellent chapter "The Moral Universe of Leaders," in Michael Genovese, *Memo to a New President* (New York: Oxford University Press, 2008), pp. 81–89.

15. I rely here on *The American Heritage Dictionary of the English Language* (Boston: Houghton Mifflin, 1969), p. 305.

16. Jonathan Alter, *The Defining Moment* (New York: Simon and Schuster, 2006), p. 336. On this same point see Isaiah Berlin, *Personal Impressions* (New York: Viking, 1981), p. 26, and Conrad Black, *Franklin Delano Roosevelt: Champion of Freedom* (New York: Public Affairs, 2003), ch. 25.

17. Gordon Brown, *Courage: Eight Portraits* (London: Bloomsbury, 2007). See also Robert Coles. *Lives of Moral Leadership* (New York: Random House, 2000).

18. Henry Fairlie, *The Life of Politics* (New York: Basic Books, 1968), p. 53.

19. Ibid., p. 55.

20. Theodore Roosevelt, *An Autobiography* (New York: Macmillan, 1913), p. 63.

21. Quoted in James MacGregor Burns and Susan Dunn, *The Three Roosevelts* (New York: Atlantic Monthly Press, 2001), p. 11.

22. Hugh Sidey, "Majesty in a Democracy," *Time*, December 1, 1980, p. 18.

23. Reagan quote from Jeffrey H. Birnbaum and Alan S. Murray, *Showdown at Gucci Gulch: Lawmakers, Lobbyists, and the Unlikely Triumph of Tax Reform* (New York: Vintage, 1988), p. 289. The Reagan optimism and impact are nicely captured in Peggy Noonan, *What I Saw at the Revolution* (New York: Random House, 1990), and Sean Wilentz, *The Age of Reagan: 1974–2008* (New York: HarperCollins, 2008).

24. On this point see especially David McCullough's *1776* (New York: Simon and Schuster, 2005).

25. Niccolò Machiavelli, *The Prince*, ed. by Harvey C. Mansfield (Chicago: University of Chicago Press, 1998), p. 58.

26. Arthur Miller, *On Politics and the Art of Acting* (New York: Viking, 2002), p. 57.

27. Fred Greenstein, *The Presidential Difference* (New York: Free Press, 2000), p. 200.

28. Orrin Hatch, *Square Peg: Confessions of a Citizen Senator* (New York: Basic Books, 2002), p. 44.

29. Liberian president Ellen Johnson-Sirleaf interview, "Dialogue," in *The Aspen Idea* (Summer 2007): p. 43. See, too, the powerful PBS documentary *The Iron Ladies of Liberia*, March 18, 2008.

30. For a classic case study of an imperfect "massive halfway" reform effort, see Birnbaum and Murray, *Showdown at Gucci Gulch*.

31. Burns and Dunn, *The Three Roosevelts,* p. 225.

32. See, on this point, Graham Allison, *The Essence of Decision* (Boston: Little, Brown, 1971). Niccolò Machiavelli famously warned leaders to shun flatterers and choose their advisers carefully. See his *The Prince,* ch. 23. See also Theodore C. Sorensen, *Decision-Making in the White House* (New York: Columbia University Press, 1963).

33. Clinton Rossiter, *The American Presidency* (New York: Mento Books, 1960), pp. 102–103.

34. Thomas E. Cronin, "All The World's a Stage—Acting and the Art of Political Leadership," *Leadership Quarterly* (Fall 2008). For a different perspective, see Gene Healy, *The Cult of the Presidency: America's Dangerous Devotion to Executive Power* (Washington, DC: Cato Institute, 2008).

35. Eco, interviewed by Deborah Soloman, "Media Studies," *New York Times Magazine*, November 25, 2007, p. 22.

36. See Doris Kearns Goodwin, *Team of Rivals: The Political Genius of Abraham Lincoln* (New York: Simon & Schuster, 2005). See also the discussion of how General George Washington recruited and promoted a number of young generals who enabled him to plan and execute major military victories in the American Revolution in McCullough, *1776*.

37. This lesson is emphasized in Jim Collins, *From Good to Great* (New York: HarperCollins, 2001).

38. For useful, if contrasting, essays on this topic see Henry Steele Commager, "Our Greatest Presidents," *Parade*, May 8, 1977, pp. 16–17, and Nelson W. Polsby, "Against Presidential Greatness," *Commentary* (January 1977): 61–64. See also Thomas A. Bailey, *Presidential Greatness* (New York: Appleton-Century, 1966), and Robert K. Murray and Tim H. Blessing, *Greatness in the White House,* 2nd ed. (University Park: Pennsylvania State University Press, 1994).

Chapter 2

1. Garry Wills, *Lincoln at Gettysburg: The Words That Remade America* (New York: Simon & Schuster, 1992), pp. 148, 175.

2. See David McCullough, *1776* (New York: Simon & Schuster, 2005), and James Thomas Flexner, *Washington: The Indispensable Man* (Boston: Little, Brown, 1974).

3. Abraham Lincoln, Annual Message to Congress, December 1, 1862, in *Lincoln: Speeches, Letters …* (New York: The Library of America, 1989), p. 415.

4. See Daniel D. Stid, *The President as Statesman* (Lawrence: University Press of Kansas, 1998).

5. Woodrow Wilson, *Constitutional Government in the United States* (New York: Columbia University Press, 1908), reproduced in Michael A. Genovese, ed., *Encyclopedia of the American Presidency* (New York: Facts on File, 2004), p. 498.

6. Peggy Noonan, *What I Saw at the Revolution* (New York: Random House, 1990), p. 69.

7. I wrote about this problem in my *The State of the Presidency* (Boston: Little, Brown, 1975). Gene Healy's *The Cult of the Presidency* (Washington, DC: Cato Institute, 2008) expands on this concern.

8. Arthur M. Schlesinger Jr., *The Imperial Presidency* (Boston: Houghton Mifflin, 1973), p. 411. He returned to this theme during George W. Bush's war on terrorism in his *War and the American Presidency* (New York: W. W. Norton, 2004).

9. In writing this chapter, I benefited from these additioinal writers and their scholarship: James David Barber, Robert N. Bellah, Daniel J. Boorstein, John Milton Cooper Jr., Clifford Geertz, Doris Kearns

Goodwin, Fred I. Greenstein, Michael Horner, Michael Novak, Stephen Oates, Michael Walzer, and Ann Ruth Willner.

Chapter 3

1. John W. Gardner, *No Easy Victories* (New York: Harper & Row, 1968), p. 84.

2. See, for examples, the classic case study by Anthony Lewis, *Gideon's Trumpet* (New York: Random House, 1964), and Jeffrey Toobin's *The Nine: Inside the Secret World of the Supreme Court* (New York: Doubleday, 2007).

3. See Martha J. Kumar and Terry Sullivan, eds., *White House World: Transitions, Organizations, and Office Operations* (College Station: Texas A&M Press, 2003). See also Charles E. Walcott and Karen M. Hult, "White House Structure and Decision Making: Elaborating the Standard Model," *Presidential Studies Quarterly* (June 2005): 303-318.

4. George W. Bush, for example, was plainly ill-informed about Iraq, both in his 2000 presidential campaign, and, more important, even when he had to make major policy decisions about invading and occupying that country. See Michael R. Gordon and General Bernard E. Trainor, *Cobra II: The Inside Story of the Invasion and Occupation of Iraq* (New York: Pantheon, 2006), and Bob Woodward, *State of Denial: Bush at War, Part III* (New York: Simon and Schuster, 2006).

5. Irving Janis, *Victims of Groupthink* (Boston: Houghton Mifflin, 1972). See also Alexander L. George, *Presidential Decisionmaking in Foreign Policy* (Boulder, CO: Westview, 1980), and Paul A. Kowert, *Groupthink or Deadlock: When Do Leaders Learn from Their Advisors?* (Albany: State University of New York Press, 2002).

6. Theodore C. Sorensen, *Decision-Making in the White House* (New York: Columbia University Press, 1963), p. 62.

7. See James P. Pfiffner, "Intelligence and Decision Making Before the War with Iraq," in George C. Edwards III and Desmond S. King, eds., *The Polarized Presidency of George W. Bush* (New York: Oxford University Press, 2007), pp. 213–242. And see James P. Pfiffner, "Presidential Decision-Making: Rationality, Advisory Systems and Personality," *Presidential Studies Quarterly* (June 2005): 217–228. See also, for a con-

troversial insider's account, Scott McClellan, *What Happened: Inside the Bush White House and Washington's Culture of Deception* (New York: Public Affairs, 2008).

8. Arthur M. Schlesinger Jr., *Crisis of Confidence: Ideas, Power, and Violence in America* (New York: Houghton Mifflin 1969), pp. 57–58.

9. For a study of a few intellectuals who did serve in the White House, see Tevi Troy, *Intellectuals and the American Presidency* (Lanham, MD: Roman and Littlefield, 2002).

10. Walter Lippmann. "The Deepest Issues of Our Time," in *Vital Speeches*, July 1, 1936.

11. Alexander Solzhenitsyn, Nobel Prize Address, 1970. A splendid example of this tradition is Elie Wiesel's *Night* (New York: Hill and Wang, 2006), originally published in 1958. See also writings by one of America's more imaginative dissenting public intellectuals in Michael Walzer's *Thinking Politically* (New Haven, CT: Yale University Press, 2007).

12. On Thoreau, see Charles A. Madison, *Critics and Crusaders* (New York: Henry Holt, 1947).

13. Paraphrased from "Gore Vidal: His Life Is an Open Book," by Kay Mills, *Los Angeles Times*, July 15, 1984, part VIII, p. 10.

14. Woodrow Wilson, quoted in James Reston, "On Kennedy's Disenchanted Intellectuals," *New York Times*, October 7, 1961.

15. The Shelley quote comes from his famous essay "In Defence of Poetry," cited in William M. Gibson, *Theodore Roosevelt Among the Humorists: W. D. Howells, Mark Twain, and Mr. Dooley* (Knoxville: University of Tennessee Press, 1980).

16. Solzhenitsyn, Nobel Prize Speech, 1970.

17. See Martha J. Kumar, *Managing the President's Message: The People, Policies, and Politics Behind the Chief Executive's Message* (Baltimore: Johns Hopkins University Press, 2007), and Lawrence R. Jacobs, "The Promotional Presidency and the New Institutional Toryism." in Edwards and King, eds., *The Polarized Presidency of George W. Bush,* pp. 285–324.

18. See Thomas R. Wolanin, *Presidential Advisory Commissions* (Madison: University of Wisconsin Press, 1975).

19. See, for example, Martha Derthick, *Policymaking for Social Security* (Washington, DC: Brookings Institution, 1979).

20. See Philip Shenon, *The Commission: The Uncensored History of the 9/11 Investigation* (New York: Twelve, 2008), and the original report, Lee Hamilton and Thomas Kean, *The 9/11 Commission Report* (New York: Norton, 2004).

21. Brent Scowcroft, "Getting the Middle East Back on Our Side," *New York Times*, January 4, 2007. See also *The Iraq Study Report* (New York: Vintage Books, 2006).

22. Jim Ruttenberg and David E. Sanger, "Bush Aides Seek Alternatives to Iraq Study Group's Proposals, Calling Them Impractical," *New York Times*, December 10, 2006, p. 18.

23. James L. Sundquist, "Research Brokerage: The Weak Link," *Brookings Institution Reprint Series* 342 (1978): 127.

24. James P. Pfiffner, "Intelligence and Decision Making Before the War with Iraq," in Edwards and King, eds., *The Polarized Presidency of George W. Bush*, p. 236.

25. Sophocles, *The Theban Plays* (Middlesex, England: Penguin, 1947).

26. Statement by Egil Krogh Jr., released by his attorney after he was sentenced in federal court for breaking the law while on the White House staff, *New York Times*, January 25, 1974, p. 16.

Chapter 4

Portions of this chapter in an earlier version were given as a keynote address at a Hofstra University conference on the John F. Kennedy presidency and published as the introductory essay in Paul Harper and Joann P. Krieg, eds., *John F. Kennedy: The Promise Revisited* (New York: Greenwood Press, 1988).

1. John Steinbeck, *America and Americans* (New York: Bonanza Books, 1966), p. 46.

2. William Manchester, *One Brief Shining Moment: Remembering Kennedy* (Boston: Little, Brown, 1983), pp. 276–277.

3. John F. Kennedy, address at Amherst College, October 26, 1963.

4. *New York Times/CBS News* Poll, July 11–13, 1996.

5. Hugh Sidey, *John F. Kennedy, President* (New York: Athenaeum, 1964), p. 11.

6. Kennedy quoted from his October 26, 1963, address about poet Robert Frost at Amherst College in Massachusetts, in Arthur M. Schlesinger Jr., *A Thousand Days: John F. Kennedy in the White House* (Boston: Houghton Mifflin, 1965), p. 1015.

7. Lawrence O'Brien, *No Final Victories* (New York: Ballantine Books, 1974), p. 2.

8. Charles Bartlett, "John F. Kennedy: The Man," in Kenneth W. Thompson, ed., *The Kennedy Presidency* (Lanham, MD: University Press of America, 1985), p. 3.

9. James MacGregor Burns, *Running Alone: Presidential Leadership JFK to Bush II* (New York: Basic Books, 2006), p. 33.

10. Richard Whalen, *The Founding Father* (New York: New American Library, 1964), p. 419. See also the portrait of Joseph Kennedy in Peter Collier and David Horowitz, *The Kennedys* (New York: Warner Books, 1984).

11. Lawrence O'Brien, *No Final Victories* (New York: Ballantine Books, 1974), p. 32.

12. Eleanor Roosevelt, quoted in J. D. Barber, *The Presidential Character* (Englewood Cliffs, NJ: Prentice-Hall, 1972), p. 295. See, too, Ted Sorensen's candid account of how and why Kennedy ducked the McCarthy issue, in his *Counselor* (New York: HarperCollins, 2008), pp 152–155.

13. Remarks of Senator John F. Kennedy, Stuyvesant Town Rally, New York, October 27, 1960, in *The Speeches of John F. Kennedy, Presidential Campaign of 1960* (Committee on Commerce, U.S. Senate, Washington, DC: U.S. Government Printing Office, 1961), p. 775.

14. John F. Kennedy (senator), speech at Sunnyside Gardens, Queens, New York, October 27, 1960, in ibid., pp. 782–783.

15. Transcript of televised address to the Greater Houston Ministerial Association, September 12, 1960.

16. See George C. Edwards, *Why The Electoral College Is Bad for America* (New Haven, CT: Yale University Press, 2004), pp. 64–67.

17. See Robert Dallek, *An Unfinished Life: John F. Kennedy* (Boston: Little, Brown, 2003).

18. See Seymour M. Hersh, *The Dark Side of Camelot* (Boston: Little, Brown, 1997). One of JFK's closest aides acknowledges that Kennedy was "self-indulgent" and "carefree" in this regard, yet says he

knows of no occasion where Kennedy's private life interfered with his public duties. Sorensen, *Counselor*, pp. 122–123.

19. Katherine Graham, *Personal History* (New York: Vintage Books, 1998), p. 290.

20. Ibid., p. 291.

21. See, for examples, Nick Bryant, *The Bystander* (New York: Basic Books, 2006), and Burns, *Running Alone*.

22. Arthur M. Schlesinger Jr., "JFK: The Man, the President," *Boston Globe*, October 20, 1979, in conjunction with the dedication of the John F. Kennedy Library. Similar reflections can be found throughout Ted Sorensen's revealing memoir *Counselor*.

23. James Sundquist, *Politics and Policy* (Washington, DC: Brookings Institution, 1968), p. 478.

24. Quote from Bill Adler, *The Kennedy Wit* (New York: Citadel Press, 1964), p. 49.

25. Herbert Parmet, *JFK: The Presidency of John F. Kennedy* (New York: Dial Press, 1983), p. 353.

26. Alan Shank, *Presidential Policy Leadership* (Lanham, MD: University Press of America, 1980), p. 276.

27. Carl Brauer, *John F. Kennedy and the Second Reconstruction* (New York: Columbia University Press, 1977), p. 320.

28. Carl B. Stokes, *Promise of Power: A Political Autobiography* (New York: Simon and Schuster, 1973), pp. 264–265. See also Bryant, *The Bystander*.

29. T. George Harris, "The Competent American," *Look*, November 17, 1964, reprinted in Earl Latham, ed., *J. F. Kennedy and Presidential Power* (New York: D. C. Heath, 1972), p. 126.

30. Ibid., p. 128.

31. Parmet, *JFK*, p. 354.

32. Jay David, ed., *The Kennedy Reader* (Indianapolis, IN: Bobbs-Merrill, 1967), pp. 121–130.

33. Garry Wills, *The Kennedy Imprisonment* (Boston: Little, Brown, 1981), p. 301.

34. Richard Walton, *Cold War and Counter Revolution: The Foreign Policy of John F. Kennedy* (New York: Viking Press, 1972), p. 234.

35. *I. F. Stone Weekly*, December 9, 1963.

36. Henry Fairlie, *The Kennedy Promise* (Garden City, NY: Doubleday, 1973).

37. David Halberstam, *The Best and the Brightest* (New York: Random House, 1972). See also Larry Berman, *Planning a Tragedy* (New York: W. W. Norton, 1982), ch. 2.

38. Nancy Gager Clinch, *The Kennedy Neurosis* (New York: Grosset and Dunlap, 1973), p. 13.

39. Ibid., p. 373.

40. Bruce Miroff, *Pragmatic Illusions* (New York: McKay, 1976), p. 295.

41. Arthur M. Schlesinger Jr., *Journals: 1952–2000* (New York: Penguin, 2007), pp. 160–161.

42. Robert S. McNamara, with Brian Van DeMark, *In Retrospect: The Tragedy and Lessons of Vietnam* (New York: Random House, 1995). See also the 2003 film documentary featuring McNamara, *The Fog of War.*

43. Harris Wofford, *Of Kennedys and Kings: Making Sense of the Sixties* (New York: Farrar, Straus and Giroux, 1980), p. 459.

44. James MacGregor Burns, *The Power to Lead* (New York: Simon and Schuster, 1984), p. 75.

45. Schlesinger, *A Thousand Days,* pp. 1030–1031.

46. Dallek, *An Unfinished Life,* p. 711. For a similar favorable view, see Sorensen, *Counselor.*

Chapter 5

Portions of this chapter were published earlier in *The Presidency and the Challenge of Democracy,* edited by Michael A. Genovese and Lori Cox Han (New York: Palgrave, 2006).

1. Arthur M. Schlesinger Jr., *War and the American Presidency* (New York: W. W. Norton, 2004), p. 66.

2. See Francis Fukuyama, *America at the Crossroads* (New Haven, CT: Yale University Press, 2006), and Larry Diamond, *The Spirit of Democracy: The Struggle to Build Free Societies Throughout the World* (New York: Times Books, 2008). See also the cautionary warnings of Amy Chua, *World on Fire* (New York: Random House, 2003).

3. See, for example, Philip Bobbitt, *Terror and Consent* (New York: Knopf, 2008), and Philippe Sands, *Torture Team: Rumsfeld's Memo and the Betrayal of American Values* (New York: Palgrave Macmillan, 2008).

4. See Peter Irons, *War Powers: How The Imperial Presidency Hijacked the Constitution* (New York: Metropolitan Books, 2005); Charlie Savage, *Takeover: The Return of the Imperial Presidency and the Subversion of American Democracy* (Boston: Little, Brown, 2007); Louis Fisher, *Presidential War Power* (Lawrence: University Press of Kansas, 2004); and Gene Healy, *The Cult of the Presidency* (Washington, DC: Cato Institute, 2008).

5. *Hamdan v. Rumsfeld*, 548 U.S. 557 (2006). See also *Boumediene v. Bush* (2008).

6. Gaillard Hunt, ed., *The Writings of James Madison*, vol. 6 (New York: Putnam, 1900–1910), p. 174.

7. Scott Gordon. *Controlling the State: Constitutionalism from Ancient Athens to Today* (Cambridge, MA: Harvard University Press, 1999), p. 361.

8. Anthony Lewis, "A President Beyond the Law," *New York Times*, May 7, 2004, p. A25. See also *Guantánamo and Beyond: The Continuing Pursuit of Unchecked Power* (Report of U.S. Amnesty International, May 2005), Jack Goldsmith, *The Terror Presidency* (New York: W. W. Norton, 2007), and David Gray Adler, "George Bush and the Abuse of History," *UCLA Journal of International Law and Foreign Affairs* (Spring 2007): 75–144.

9. Elizabeth Poroledo, "Italian Leader Chastises U.S. in Kidnapping Case in Milan," *New York Times*, July 2, 2005, p. A4. See also William G. Weaver and Robert M. Pallitto, "'Extraordinary Rendition' and Presidential Fiat," *Presidential Studies Quarterly* (March 2006): 102–116.

10. Louis Fisher, "From Presidential Wars to American Hegemony: The Constitution after 9/11," in Michael A. Genovese and Lori Cox Han, eds., *The Presidency and the Challenge of Democracy* (New York: Palgrave MacMillan, 2006), p. 23. See also Peter Irons, *War Powers* (New York: Metropolitan, 2005).

11. Schlesinger, *War and the American Presidency,* p. 66.

12. See, in general, John Bolton, *Surrender Is Not an Option: Defending America at the United Nations and Abroad* (New York: Threshold, 2008).

13. Goldsmith, *The Terror Presidency*, p. 205.

14. See the analysis of the backlash and polarization this caused in Gary C. Jacobson, *A Divider Not a Uniter* (New York: Pearson, 2007), and George C. Edwards III and Desmond S. King, eds., *The Polarized*

Presidency of George W. Bush (New York: Oxford University Press, 2007). See also Scott McClellan, *What Happened: Inside the Bush White House and Washington's Culture of Deception* (New York: Public Affairs, 2008).

15. See, for examples, David Gray Adler and Larry N. George, eds., *The Constitution and the Conduct of American Foreign Policy* (Lawrence: University Press of Kansas, 1996), and David Gray Adler and Michael Genovese, eds., *The Presidency and the Law* (Lawrence: University Press of Kansas, 2002).

16. See Clinton Rossiter, *Constitutional Dictatorship* (New York: Harcourt, Brace, 1948); James MacGregor Burns, *Presidential Government* (Boston: Houghton Mifflin, 1966); and Terry Eastland, *Energy in the Executive: The Case for a Strong Presidency* (New York: Free Press, 1992). For contrarian thoughts, see Healy, *The Cult of the Presidency.*

17. Clinton Rossiter, *Constitutional Dictatorship: Crisis Government in the Modern Democracies* (Princeton, NJ: Princeton University Press, 1948), p. 314.

18. John Yoo, *War by Other Means* (New York: Atlantic Monthly Press, 2006), p. 103.

19. Ibid.

20. Richard A. Posner, *Not a Suicide Pact: The Constitution in a Time of National Emergency* (New York: Oxford University Press, 2006), p. 1.

21. Ibid., p. 15.

22. Arthur M. Schlesinger Jr., "Foreword," in Adler and George, eds., *The Constitution and the Conduct of American Foreign Policy*, p. xi. See also the helpful historical perspective provided in Edward S. Corwin, *Total War and the Constitution* (New York: Knopf, 1947).

23. On these issues, see Howard Ball, *Bush, the Detainees, and the Constitution* (Lawrence: University Press of Kansas, 2007).

24. See Posner, *Not A Suicide Pact,* ch. 3.

25. James Risen, *State of War: The Secret History of the CIA and the Bush Administration* (New York: Free Press, 2006).

26. See Goldsmith, *The Terror Presidency,* ch. 5.

27. See Savage, *Takeover*, ch. 10. See also Phillip J. Cooper, "George W. Bush, Edgar Allen Poe, and the Use and Abuse of Presidential Signing Statements," *Presidential Studies Quarterly* (September 2005): 515–532.

28. Tony Judt, "The New World Order," *New York Review of Books,* July 14, 2005, pp. 17–18.

29. Michael R. Gordan and Bernard E. Trainor, *Cobra II* (New York: Pantheon, 2006), and Michael Isikoff and David Corn, *Hubris* (New York: Crown, 2006).

30. See James Fallows, "Blind into Baghdad," *Atlantic Monthly* (January/February 2004); Larry Diamond, "What Went Wrong in Iraq," *Foreign Affairs* (September/October 2004); and David C. Hendrickson and Robert W. Tucker, "Revisions in Need of Revising: What Went Wrong in the Iraq War," *Survival* (Summer 2005). See also, for a broader context, Samuel P. Huntington, *The Clash of Civilizations and the Remaking of World Order* (New York: Simon and Schuster, 1996), and Anthony Shadid, *Night Draws Near: Iraq's People in the Shadow of America's War* (New York: Holt, 2005).

31. Presidential signing statement of H.R. 2863. quoted in Goldsmith, *The Terror Presidency*, p. 86.

32. David Gray Adler, "George Bush and the Abuse of History: The Constitution and Presidential Power in Foreign Affairs," *UCLA Journal of International Law and Foreign Affairs* (Spring 2007): 78–79.

33. Savage, *Takeover*, pp. 329–330. See also James P. Pfiffner, *Power Play: The Bush Presidency and the Constitution* (Washington, DC: Brookings Institution, 2008), ch. 8.

34. Cited in Savage, *Takeover*, p. 330. From *Korematsu v. United States*, 321 U.S. 760 (1944).

35. Quoted in Keith Perine, "Court Rulings Erode Base of Imprisonment Policy," *Congressional Quarterly*, March 7, 2005, p. 555. See also Neil A. Lewis, "Judge Says U.S. Terror Suspect Can't Be Held as an Enemy Combatant," *New York Times*, March 1, 2005, p. A14.

36. O'Connor in *Hamdan v. Rumsfeld*, 548 U.S. 557 (2006).

37. See Ball, *Bush, the Detainees, and the Constitution.*

38. Goldsmith, *The Terror Presidency*, p. 211.

39. Editorial, "Fighting for Our Values," *Los Angeles Times*, September 28, 2005, p. B12.

40. Joseph L. Galloway, "Hold Brass Accountable," *Monterey County Herald*, September 30, 2005, p. A10.

41. See Fareed Zakaria, *The Post-American World* (New York: W. W. Norton, 2008).

42. Robert W. Tucker and David C. Hendrickson, "The Sources of American Legitimacy," *Foreign Affairs* (November/December 2004): 32.

See also Andrew J. Bacevich, *The New American Militarism: How Americans Are Seduced by War* (New York: Oxford University Press, 2005).

43. Amy Chua, untitled essay, *The Washington Monthly* (January/February/March 2008): 24.

44. Arthur M. Schlesinger Jr., in Gabor S. Boritt, ed., *Lincoln, The War President* (Gettysburg, PA: Gettysburg Civil War Institute, 1992), p. 326.

45. See a defense of the United Nations and its human rights and peacekeeping potential in Samantha Power's biography *Chasing the Flame: Segio Vieira and the Fight to Save the World* (New York: Penguin, 2008).

46. Senator Robert Taft, December 19, 1941, *From the Papers of Robert Taft* (Kent, OH: Kent State University Press, 1997), p. 303.

47. James A. Baker and Warren Christopher, "Put War Powers Back Where They Belong," *New York Times,* July 8, 2008, p. A23.

48. "Editorial: Horrifying and Unnecessary," *New York Times,* March 2, 2008, p. 10.

49. Justice David Davis in *Ex Parte Milligan*, 71 U.S. 2 (1886).

50. Quoted in Linda Greenhouse, "Detainees in Cuba Win Major Ruling in Supreme Court," *New York Times,* June 13, 2008, pp. 1, 20.

51. *Olmstead v. United States*, 277 U.S. 438 (1928).

52. *Youngstown Sheet and Tube Co. v. Sawyer*, 343 U.S. 579 (1952).

53. "High Court Moves toward Justice," *Gazette* (Colorado Springs), June 14, 2008, p. A18. See Pfiffner, *Power Play*, ch. 5.

54. Useful primers for future presidents and their advisers are: Alexander L. George, *On Foreign Policy: Unfinished Business* (Boulder, CO: Paradigm Publishers, 2006); Michael A. Genovese, *Memo to a New President* (New York: Oxford University Press, 2007); Madeleine Albright, *Memo to the President Elect* (New York: HarperCollins, 2008); and David M. Abshire, *A Call to Greatness: Challenging Our Next President* (Lanham, MD: Rowman and Littlefield, 2008); plus the already cited writings of Louis Fisher, James Pfiffner, and Arthur M. Schlesinger Jr.

Index

About the Author

Tom Cronin is the McHugh Professor of American Institutions and Leadership at Colorado College. He is president emeritus of Whitman College (1993–2005) and a former acting president of Colorado College (1991).

Cronin served as a White House Fellow on the White House staff in the mid-1960s and later was a scholar in residence at the Brookings Institution, the Center for the Study of Democratic Institutions, and the Hoover Institution.

He earned his Ph.D. in political science from Stanford University and is author, coauthor, or editor of 12 books on American politics and government. He served as president of both the Western Political Science Association and the American Political Science Association's Presidency Research Group. He has been a moderator of 15 Aspen Institute Executive Seminars, and is a frequent commentator on the presidency and presidential elections. He can be reached at tom.cronin@colorado.college.edu.